THE
GOOD PLACE
ORGANIZATION

A LEADER'S GUIDE TO STEWARDING GOOD PLACE ORGANIZATIONS

Scripture quotations are from the ESV® Bible (The Holy Bible, English Standard Version®), Copyright © 2001 by Crossway, a publishing ministry of Good News Publishers. Used by permission. All rights reserved.

The Good Place Organization
A Leader's Guide to Stewarding Good Place Organizations:

Published by Good Place Publishing
4835 Darrow Rd, Stow, OH 44224
https://goodplaceholdings.com/

Illustrations by: Chris Young and Chris Taylor, Taylor'd Design

Printed in the United States of America.

ISBN: 978-0-939320-51-6

TESTIMONIALS

FOR THE BOOK AND THE INSTITUTE

"As someone who has spent my career helping company leaders align their faith with their work in building their company, I have become immersed in the Good Place principles, values, and processes, having implemented them for more than a decade. I cannot emphasize enough how much these truths, and more importantly the vision and organization that can come when applying these truths, build a company seamlessly integrating faith and success in business. Chris has captured the essence of Good Place, connecting scriptural truth to leading and operating a Kingdom company. You will be blessed. You might even be changed."

Alan Ross, CEO
Kingdom Companies

"This is a fantastic read! It is written by authors who lead a Good Place organization and are actively helping both not-for-profit and for-profit organizations become Good Place organizations! This biblically based book is a comprehensive look at Good Place organizations. It provides the what, why, and how to leading a Good Place organization. I pray for more Good Place organizations in this world!"

Vice President, a Fortune 250 company and
Board Chair, a City Movement Non-Profit

"Akron Hardware was a $50+ million wholesale distributor of door hardware headquartered in Akron, OH with distribution facilities in 6 states (Akron Hardware was purchased in 2017). Our 85 employees were always a very important and appreciated part of our success. We brought Chris Young in to facilitate and lead some strategic planning, vision casting, team building sessions over the span of a few years. Chris has an exceptional skill at creating an inclusive and safe environment that encourages employees of all levels to participate. The sessions were also very productive and efficient, utilizing techniques that we could repeat in various settings as appropriate. We came away with valuable and actionable input that helped us form and refine our plans for greater success. We would highly recommend Chris and his organization."

Tom Orihel, Former Chief Operating Officer
Akron Hardware

"Essential! As a teacher and author, I'm not necessarily business oriented. The thought of creating a business plan for a new organization was overwhelming- and honestly a bit terrifying. Chris Young with The Good Place Institute guided me step-by-step simplifying the process. In our initial meeting, he presented an overview and clearly explained the different parts to a charter and business plan. Next, in order to draft a personalized plan relevant to my organization, Chris constructed the template, asked pertinent questions, and assigned weekly "homework." Using the depth of his experience with much larger organizations, he shared formative thoughts and strategic ideas that rounded out the process. In a matter of weeks, I held a professional plan in my hands ready to share with others! Working with Chris has been tremendously beneficial. I highly recommend."

Carmen Beasley, Founder and Author
Simply Bible

"We engaged with The Good Place Institute as we were looking to create a greater impact for what we do. From our perspective, simply applying traditional strategic planning was not enough to produce the value we wanted. After working with GPI, we changed the way we conducted our business to better value our people allowing them to flourish, we became better aware of our internal systems and their interactions, becoming more profitable but also positively impacting our clients, our stakeholders, and the communities where we do business. This has been a journey we have enjoyed, and we look forward to continue progressing, experiencing shalom every step of the way."

Miguel Gomez, Senior Managing Director
Transom Group – Americas

"When we were developing our 3-year strategic plan we worked with Chris and Good Place Holdings. The structure and flexibility Chris gave me to lead, but also partake in the process was a blessing as I was learning myself. He didn't try to force his system or way of thinking but allowed myself and the leadership to think about who we are and the impact we are working to make. Chris also hosted a board retreat that allowed our board to engage in the dreaming and build buy-in for years to come."

Zac Kohl, Executive Director
The Well Community Development Corporation

THE
GOOD PLACE
ORGANIZATION

Your word is a lamp to my feet and a light to my path.

Psalm 119:105

Your kingdom come, Your will be done, on earth as it is in heaven.

Matthew 6:10

But seek first the kingdom of God and his righteousness, and all these things will be added to you.

Matthew 6:33

In Him we live and move and have our being.

Acts 17:28a

And whatever you do, in word or deed, do everything in the name of the Lord Jesus, giving thanks to God the Father through him.

Colossians 3:17

CONTENTS

THE AUTHORS

Scott Myers

Scott is the Chair of the Board of Good Place Holdings and author of the philosophy and principles of Good Place through his writings in the The Eutopia Book series (Good Place Publishing, 2017) and The Art of Life in Organizations: Finding Value (Good Place Publishing, 2005). Scott has spent over three decades researching and building up organizations locally, nationally, and internationally, in the for-profit and non-profit sectors based on what the God of the Bible says about good places, work, life in organizations to build up hearts of love, lives of shalom, making the world a better place. Scott holds a Bachelor of Arts in Humanities from Houghton College.

Dale Bissonette

Dale is the President of Good Place Holdings and the CEO of SD Myers, Inc. (a Good Place Holdings company). Dale has been leading local, national, and international organizations in the for-profit and non-profit sectors based on Biblical principles and values for over thirty years in such roles as Owner, CEO, President, Board Chair and Member, and CFO. Dale holds a Bachelor of Science in Accounting from The University of Akron.

Chris Young

Chris is the President of The Good Place Institute (a Good Place Holdings organization) and former Chief of Staff at Good Place Holdings. Chris has spent over twenty years researching and developing Biblically based approaches, methods, and resources, while leading and helping others build and steward for-profit and non-profit organizations to bring about organizational life and achieve organizational success from a Biblical worldview. Chris holds a Bachelor of Science in Business Management from Canisius College and a Master of Arts in Religion from Trinity International University (Trinity Evangelical Divinity School).

CHAPTER 1

INTRODUCTION AND FORMAT

This book is meant to be a practical guide for leaders who are interested in knowing more or are on the journey of leading and building Good Place organizations. The organization could be for-profit or non-profit, big or small, privately or publicly held, from Main Street to Wall Street. Good Places have their purpose, foundation, characteristics, outworking, and success criteria derived from and rooted in the principles and values of the God of the Bible and His Word. The God of the Bible is described in its pages as trinitarian—meaning one God in three persons: Father, Son, and Holy Spirit (Deuteronomy 6:4; Matthew 28:19; John 1:1; 1 Corinthians 8:6; 2 Corinthians 13:14; Ephesians 4:30; Colossians 2:9). God is eternal (Revelation 22:13), creator of all things (Genesis 1:1, Colossians 1:16), the giver of life (John 1:1–8), omniscient (Psalm 147:5, 1 John 3:20), omnipresent (Psalm 139:7–10), omnipotent (Job 42:1–2), unchanging (Hebrews 13:8), holy, (1 Peter 1:16; Revelation 4:8), righteous (Deuteronomy 32:4; Psalm 145:17), just (Psalm 106:3), gracious and merciful (Psalm 103:8; Ephesians 2:4–5; Hebrews 4:16), and love (1 John 4:8, 16).

God's Word comes through the Bible (the inspired and inerrant Word of God), through Jesus (the Word made flesh), and through creation (spoken into existence with purpose and designed properties by God's Word). For a Good Place, and this book, we look to the Bible because it is the information source and worldview lens that we have been given in our age through which to view the world and everything in it for an accurate picture of true reality as designed and purposed by its Creator and Author.

As we journey through this guide together, we aim to be aware of the storyline (or metanarrative) of the Bible in such a way as to understand and engage in the purposes, principles, and values derived from the Bible and apply them through specific methods and tools to organizational life to build up Good Place organizations. As we do, we will encounter many themes and consistencies. We will encounter words and topics that can be used to describe and that will be found throughout the framework of Good Place, Good Place principles and values, and the methods and tools as they are applied. The first theme is **love**. God is love. God first loved us. The Great Commandment is to love God and love people (Matthew 22:36–40). There is no greater love than someone laying down their life for their friends (John 15:13). We are asked to speak truth in love (Ephesians 4:15). We are also told that we can say and do a lot of things, but if we do not have love, we are nothing more than a noisy gong or clanging cymbal (1 Corinthians 13:1). We are called to love through serving one another (Galatians 5:13). Love should motivate, cover, and permeate all we do.

A close relative of love is **humility**. It is impossible to love the way God tells us to love without humility. We are to operate with gentleness and humility, with patience, bearing with one another in love (Ephesians 4:2). We are told to do nothing from pride or selfish ambition, but to humble ourselves and think of others as more significant, looking not only to our own interests but also to the interests of others, and in so doing be unified and of one mind (Philippians 2:2–4).

Another theme we encounter is **stewardship**. We are all called to be good stewards of that which God has entrusted to us, whether that be ourselves, those we lead, material things, organizations, processes, resources, skills, talents, etc. God is looking for us to manage and invest well that which He has given to us to steward and give a return (to Him, the Owner of all things), building on, developing, enhancing, and improving those things He has given and entrusted to us (Matthew 25:14–30).

Another theme is **purpose**. Purpose in the sense of why are we here: Why do we exist, and what is our aim? For instance, the Westminster Shorter Catechism states that the chief end of people is to glorify God and enjoy Him forever. Everything God created, and especially the pinnacle of His creation, human beings, has a purpose and was designed with an aim in mind.

Other themes we will encounter are **connectedness** and **coherence**, in the sense that we and everything we do is connected to and has coherence in relationship to God, to purpose, and to each other. And as we will find later in this book, the methods and tools we have developed to bring about Good Place organizations also have intended connectedness and coherence to God and His work, to purpose, to each other, and to the aims for which they were created and/or assembled to fulfill.

Lastly, we intend to bring about and experience the theme of **shalom**, in its fullest sense in one's being, meaning peace, harmony, completeness, well-being, wholeness, fullness. Our goal is to build up hearts of love and lives of shalom. Shalom is a main characteristic of what people have in Good Places, whether that was in the Garden of Eden, the Promised Land, the Church, God's Kingdom on earth, or the future New Jerusalem (the new heavens and the new earth).

You will find these themes interwoven throughout this book and permeating the principles and values and the methods and tools as we apply them to building Good Place organizations.

In the **construct** and **format** of this book, we will first provide a Biblical foundation for Good Place, introducing Biblical narratives, principles, and concepts that have informed our perspective on work, organizational life, and the concept of Good Place and Good Place organizations. In chapters 2 through 8, we discuss the Bible, a brief storyline of the Bible, where we find good places in the Bible, and the sacredness and purpose of work. We believe establishing this Biblical foundation and addressing the "why" is significantly important to accurately informing the "what" and the "how" that comes later.

In chapters 9 and 10 we will define and discuss Good Place and the purpose of Good Place organizations. This will inform what a Good Place is and the aim and success criteria for Good Place organizations, what we are building to achieve.

In chapter 11, we will introduce and discuss each of *The 10 Areas of Stewarding a Good Place Organization*. For each area, we will address a brief Biblical summary of the area, discuss the principles and values derived from the Bible, and provide practical leadership application of the methods and tools that have been developed, designed, and/or assembled in such a way as to serve as building blocks to build Good Place organizations and fulfill the purpose and achieve the aims of Good Place organizations. In Appendix 2 we also offer further investigation of representative Scripture from which we derive the principles and values of each of *The 10 Areas of Stewarding a Good Place Organization.*

CHAPTER 2

THE JOURNEY BEGINS

❝ Let's start at the very beginning, a very good place to start." As sung by the brilliant philosopher, Julie Andrews, who played Maria Von Trapp in the Rogers and Hammerstein 1965 musical, *The Sound of Music*.

So let's start at the beginning with a few starter questions to kick us off and set our stage:

As an individual, would you rather be in a good place or a bad place?

As an organization, would you rather work at a good place or a bad place?

As a community, would you rather live in a good place or a bad place?

For our purposes, please take these questions at face value. These are not meant to be trick questions. Hopefully, the answer to these simple questions is obvious. Hopefully, most if not all people, including someone reading this book, would choose the good place over the bad place.

If we can agree on that, we can move on to the next question:

What is a Good Place?

Before we give the answer, however, let us go to the place where we will get our premise, foundation, and definition of good and Good Place: the God of the Bible and His Word, the Bible, the life of Jesus, and creation. Therefore, the definition of good and, therefore, Good Place does not change with culture or individual opinions or feelings. It resides in God and His Word and is timeless and constant. This is where we get the principles, values, and characteristics of a Good Place. As we journey along together, you may find that you have different ideas or definitions of good, or what is a good place. As you read along in the next several chapters and we discuss the foundational elements of Good Place, please consider where we get our definition and foundation upon which we will build Good Place organizations, and why we get them from there.

You are welcome to continue reading in order, or you may opt to skip to chapters 9 and 10, which define what a Good Place is and the purpose of Good Place organizations, or jump to chapter 11, where we discuss the principles and values and begin applying the methods and tools to build up and lead a Good Place organization. Then perhaps come back to chapters 3 through 8 later to better understand the foundation upon which Good Place and *The 10 Areas* are built.

CHAPTER 3

THE FOUNDATION OF GOOD PLACE

The foundation of Good Place is found in God and His Word, the Bible, the life of Jesus, and creation.

All Scripture is breathed out by God and profitable for teaching, for reproof, for correction, and for training in righteousness, that the man of God may be complete, equipped for every good work.

2 Timothy 3:16–17

Foundational elements can be found in the life of Jesus.

And the Word became flesh and dwelt among us, and we have seen his glory, glory as of the only Son from the Father, full of grace and truth.

John 1:14

And foundational elements can also be found in God's creation.

For his invisible attributes, namely, his eternal power and divine nature, have been clearly perceived, ever since the creation of the world, in the things that have been made. So they are without excuse.

Romans 1:20

Regardless of your view of the Bible, whether you believe it is simply a historical work of literature, a depiction of history, or the actual inerrant word of God, the Bible outside of its religious context is a book (and more accurately a library of books) that has stood the test of time and significantly influenced the world in which we live. It is estimated that the Bible is the best-selling book of all time with approximately 5 billion copies sold and distributed worldwide.[1] The Bible, including its principles and values, has been used as the foundation of the most sustainable and successful governments and has shaped societies and cultures around the world for centuries, specifically Western civilization and culture.[2] Its words have changed the world and individual lives.

We do acknowledge that the Bible has also been used and applied wrongly by some to justify injustices and wrongdoing. We suggest that those who use it to justify wrongdoing do so in knowing contrast with the true storyline of the Bible or do so unknowingly because of ignorance of the true storyline.

---

1   "Best-selling book," *The Guinness Book of World Records* (Stamford, CT: Guinness Media, 1997), https://www.guinnessworldrecords.com/world-records/best-selling-book-of-non-fiction.

2   Vishal Mangalwadi, *The Book that Made Your World: How the Bible Created the Soul of Western Civilization* (Nashville: Thomas Nelson, 2011).

The Bible, and the storyline throughout, defines "good" and describes what is "good." It also describes good places. And when you apply the principles and values of God's Word, the Bible, what is produced is good and a good place.

When you apply the principles of God's Word and the Bible to individual life, to the life of an organization, or to the life of a community, what you are building and/or what will be produced is good and a good place. More on this in later sections.

CHAPTER 4

WHY THE BIBLE?

AN ARGUMENT FROM PURPOSE AND DESIGN

The foundation of Good Place and the source of Good Place principles and values is God and His Word—mainly the Bible, the life of Jesus, and creation. We have designed and/or assembled methods and tools to reflect these principles and values derived from God and His Word. But why the Bible and the God of the Bible? One way to answer this question is from the perspective of design.

If we simply look around our world, we find purpose and design. We can look specifically in nature, God's creation according to the Bible, and find so much design in our world that we humans look to it for principles to optimize our own manufactured designs. We call this *biomimicry*. For example, we can look at a sunflower and find its purpose and design. We find its purpose to be everything from simple beauty to edible seeds, to pollination, to soil enrichment. We find its design optimally distributes water and captures the sun's energy. The purpose and design we see in a sunflower led to our manufactured designs of everything from shower heads that optimally distribute water, to solar panels that optimally collect the sun's energy. We could cite innumerable examples of purpose and design found in our world.

When we find purpose and design in our world, it makes sense that there is a designer. Just like when we look at a building and we know there was an architect who designed it, or view a painting and know there was an artist who created it, both with a purpose in mind that what they created was designed to fulfill. Therefore, when we look at the world, we know there is a Designer, a Creator who had purpose for that which was designed and created. This is called the Intelligent Design Argument. It is fascinating that so often we, as reasoning human beings, will look at anything where we see purpose and design and inherently know there was an "intelligent being" who was responsible for developing it and had a purpose for developing it, except for the created world. Is there anything else in our human experience that we see and experience purpose and/or design (and even an incomprehensible range and mix of interconnectedness and dependencies) and ascribe random chance to its coming into being? The short answer is "no." We look at anything created, a thing that has purpose and design, and can reasonably conclude there was an intelligent designer who created it. Unfortunately, this small section in this guide cannot do justice to this topic. For more on this, there are many and significant materials that have been written to investigate this argument.[3]

Therefore, we put forth that it is most reasonable, and certainly makes Biblical sense, that when we see design in our world, we look to the Designer to understand its purpose. We look to the Designer for the purpose of that which has been designed and created. Therefore, we look to the Bible, which describes the Designer, the Creator of the universe and everything in it, for its purpose and what is good about it. We look to the Bible because it claims to be the Designer's words about the purpose of our world and our lives together and poses design principles and values for us to follow. If we are guided by these principles and values, led by the intended design in the life of an individual, the life of an organization, and/or the life of a community, we will be optimizing the intended design and fulfilling its purpose. What we will find ourselves building and producing is good, a Good Place.

One significant area where we see design in our world is in people—who we are, how we are made, how the body heals, how our bodies use food as energy, how we relate and thrive in the ecosystem around us that sustains human life, etc. So what does the Designer have to say about the purpose and design of people?

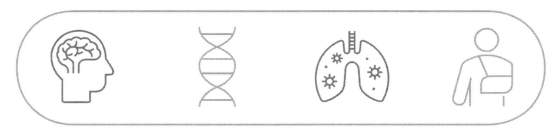

The Bible states that people were created in God's image and likeness (Genesis 1:26–27). What does this mean? This means people bear the image of the Creator God, the Designer, the Architect of all things. What is God's image, and therefore, what image do we bear? A few, but not exhaustive, thoughts on this topic include characteristics of God. He is a Creator; we are creative and have the opportunity to continue His creation. He is relational, as specifically seen in the Trinity; we are relational and were made to be in relationship with God and as social beings in relational community with one another. God is a worker, a gardener, a carpenter; we were designed to work. God is love; we are called to love one another. God is full of and extends grace, mercy, and justice; we are called to the same.

---

3   We refer you to a few of those authors and their books, including Michael Behe, Darwin's Black Box: The Biochemical Challenge to Evolution and The Edge of Evolution: The Search for the Limits of Darwinism; Stephen Meyer, Darwin's Doubt: The Explosive Origin of Animal Life and the Case for Intelligent Design, Signature in the Cell: DNA and the Evidence for Intelligent Design, and The Return of the God Hypothesis; and Philip Johnson, Darwin on Trial.

These are just a few examples. We also see in the Bible that Jesus, the God/man or God in human form, is the total, complete, and perfect embodiment of God (John 1:1, 14, 30; Colossians 2:9), and therefore, as image bearers, we look to and are to model and become more like Him.

So specifically for the purpose of this guide and for building up Good Places, we ask ourselves the following questions:

> What is a good place according to the Designer and Architect of good places?

> What is the Designer's purpose for creating good places?

> What is the overall storyline of the Bible, and what does that say about the purpose and design of human life, work, and life in an organization in these good places?

Some answers to these questions are offered in the next two chapters of this book.

CHAPTER 5

GOOD PLACE IN THE BIBLE

The Bible describes good places throughout its books and pages. Scott Myers, in his book Eutopia Book 1 Communities[4] has a wonderful way of sharing how the Bible describes these good places throughout the front, the middle, and the back of the book (or library of books if you are a theology geek). We have adapted this approach and his writings on this subject in this section to share the theological foundation of Good Place.

The Front

In the *front* of the Bible, Genesis 1:1–31, we read:

> In the beginning, God created the heavens and the earth. The earth was without form and void, and darkness was over the face of the deep. And the Spirit of God was hovering over the face of the waters.
>
> And God said, "Let there be light," and there was light. And God saw that the light was good. And God separated the light from the darkness. God called the light Day, and the darkness he called Night. And there was evening and there was morning, the first day.
>
> And God said, "Let there be an expanse in the midst of the waters, and let it separate the waters from the waters." And God made the expanse and separated the waters that were under the expanse from the waters that were above the expanse. And it was so. And God called the expanse Heaven. And there was evening and there was morning, the second day.
>
> And God said, "Let the waters under the heavens be gathered together into one place, and let the dry land appear." And it was so. God called the dry land Earth, and the waters that were gathered together he called Seas. And God saw that it was good.
>
> And God said, "Let the earth sprout vegetation, plants yielding seed, and fruit trees bearing fruit in which is their seed, each according to its kind, on the earth." And it was so. The earth brought forth vegetation, plants yielding seed according to their own kinds, and trees bearing fruit in which is their seed, each according to its kind. And God saw that it was good. And there was evening and there was morning, the third day.

---

4 Scott Myers, *The Eutopia Book: 1 Communities* (Tallmadge, OH: Good Place Publishing, 2017).

And God said, "Let there be lights in the expanse of the heavens to separate the day from the night. And let them be for signs and for seasons, and for days and years, and let them be lights in the expanse of the heavens to give light upon the earth." And it was so. And God made the two great lights—the greater light to rule the day and the lesser light to rule the night—and the stars. And God set them in the expanse of the heavens to give light on the earth, to rule over the day and over the night, and to separate the light from the darkness. And God saw that it was good. And there was evening and there was morning, the fourth day.

And God said, "Let the waters swarm with swarms of living creatures, and let birds fly above the earth across the expanse of the heavens." So God created the great sea creatures and every living creature that moves, with which the waters swarm, according to their kinds, and every winged bird according to its kind. And God saw that it was good. And God blessed them, saying, "Be fruitful and multiply and fill the waters in the seas, and let birds multiply on the earth." And there was evening and there was morning, the fifth day.

And God said, "Let the earth bring forth living creatures according to their kinds—livestock and creeping things and beasts of the earth according to their kinds." And it was so. And God made the beasts of the earth according to their kinds and the livestock according to their kinds, and everything that creeps on the ground according to its kind. And God saw that it was good.

Then God said, "Let us make man in our image, after our likeness. And let them have dominion over the fish of the sea and over the birds of the heavens and over the livestock and over all the earth and over every creeping thing that creeps on the earth."

> So God created man in his own image,
>   in the image of God he created him;
>   male and female he created them.

And God blessed them. And God said to them, "Be fruitful and multiply and fill the earth and subdue it, and have dominion over the fish of the sea and over the birds of the heavens and over every living thing that moves on the earth." And God said, "Behold, I have given you every plant yielding seed that is on the face of all the earth, and every tree with seed in its fruit. You shall have them for food. And to every beast of the earth and to every bird of the heavens and to everything that creeps on the earth, everything that has the breath of life, I have given every green plant for food." And it was so. And God saw everything that he had made, and behold, it was very good. And there was evening and there was morning, the sixth day.

In Genesis 2:4–17, we continue to read:

> These are the generations
> of the heavens and the earth when they were created,
> in the day that the Lord God made the earth and the heavens.

When no bush of the field was yet in the land and no small plant of the field had yet sprung up—for the Lord God had not caused it to rain on the land, and there was no man to work the ground, and a mist was going up from the land and was watering the whole face of the ground—then the Lord God formed the man of dust from the ground and breathed into his nostrils the breath of life, and the man became a living creature. And the Lord God planted a garden in Eden, in the east, and there he put the man whom he had formed. And out of the ground the Lord God made to spring up every tree that is pleasant to the sight and good for food. The tree of life was in the midst of the garden, and the tree of the knowledge of good and evil.

A river flowed out of Eden to water the garden, and there it divided and became four rivers. The name of the first is the Pishon. It is the one that flowed around the whole land of Havilah, where there is gold. And the gold of that land is good; bdellium and onyx stone are there. The name of the second river is the Gihon. It is the one that flowed around the whole land of Cush. And the name of the third river is the Tigris, which flows east of Assyria. And the fourth river is the Euphrates.

The Lord God took the man and put him in the garden of Eden to work it and keep it. And the Lord God commanded the man, saying, "You may surely eat of every tree of the garden, but of the tree of the knowledge of good and evil you shall not eat, for in the day that you eat of it you shall surely die."

In the *front* of the Bible, beginning with the creation story in Genesis, the Bible describes God creating—the heavens and earth; light, water, and land; vegetation; animals and living creatures; and human beings. At the end of each day of creating, God said what He had created was good. At the end of the sixth day, when His original creation was finished, He said it was very good. God created a place for us to live. He made it a place where we had everything we needed, where we could live in a way that He intended, where He could bless us, where His majesty and splendor would be on display, where He would be glorified, and where we would flourish. A *Good Place*. Unfortunately, we made choices that led to us to no longer be able to live in that Good Place.

The Middle

Further, in Genesis 12:1–3, we read:

Now the Lord said to Abram, "Go from your country and your kindred and your father's house to the land that I will show you. And I will make of you a great nation, and I will bless you and make your name great, so that you will be a blessing. I will bless those who bless you, and him who dishonors you I will curse, and in you all the families of the earth shall be blessed."

In Deuteronomy 28 and 30, we read:

> And if you faithfully obey the voice of the Lord your God, being careful to do all his commandments that I command you today, the Lord your God will set you high above all the nations of the earth. And all these blessings shall come upon you and overtake you, if you obey the voice of the Lord your God. (Deuteronomy 28:1–2)

> But if you will not obey the voice of the Lord your God or be careful to do all his commandments and his statutes that I command you today, then all these curses shall come upon you and overtake you. (Deuteronomy 28:15)

> If you obey the commandments of the Lord your God that I command you today, by loving the Lord your God, by walking in his ways, and by keeping his commandments and his statutes and his rules, then you shall live and multiply, and the Lord your God will bless you in the land that you are entering to take possession of it. (Deuteronomy 30:16)

In Exodus, the land is described this way:

> And I have come down to deliver them out of the hand of the Egyptians and to bring them up out of that land to a good and broad land, a land flowing with milk and honey…(Exodus 3:8)

God chose the descendants of Abraham (the people of Israel), had them live in a good place, and gave them a way to live that God could bless. The purpose was so that as they lived that way and flourished in that good place, God would bless them and everyone would see it and desire to live in the same way, glorifying God and living life as He intends. Unfortunately, that did not work out either, and many of them settled in other areas besides this Promised Land.

Also, in the Old Testament section of the Bible, in 1 Kings 10:1–9, we read about Solomon, his wisdom, and his kingdom:

> Now when the queen of Sheba heard of the fame of Solomon concerning the name of the Lord, she came to test him with hard questions. She came to Jerusalem with a very great retinue, with camels bearing spices and very much gold and precious stones. And when she came to Solomon, she told him all that was on her mind. And Solomon answered all her questions; there was nothing hidden from the king that he could not explain to her. And when the queen of Sheba had seen all the wisdom of Solomon, the house that he had built, the food of his table, the seating of his officials, and the attendance of his servants, their clothing, his cupbearers, and his burnt offerings that he offered at the house of the Lord, there was no more breath in her.

And she said to the king, "The report was true that I heard in my own land of your words and of your wisdom, but I did not believe the reports until I came and my own eyes had seen it. And behold, the half was not told me. Your wisdom and prosperity surpass the report that I heard. Happy are your men! Happy are your servants, who continually stand before you and hear your wisdom! Blessed be the Lord your God, who has delighted in you and set you on the throne of Israel! Because the Lord loved Israel forever, he has made you king, that you may execute justice and righteousness."

Solomon asked God for wisdom, and God granted him wisdom and a discerning heart, plus all that he did not ask including incomparable riches and honor. So much so that people around the world took notice and one, in this story, came to visit and see if all she had heard about Solomon and his kingdom was true. Solomon led his people with wisdom and discernment, governing and stewarding well all that the Lord had given to him so that God was glorified and the people of the kingdom flourished.

Hundreds of years later, in chapter 2 of the New Testament Book of Acts, Peter's message on the day of Pentecost was heard in the languages of people from many nations who had come to Jerusalem to celebrate the Jewish festival of Pentecost. No doubt many of them were ethnic Jews who had moved and settled in other nations and were returning for the celebration. Some of them also were people from other nationalities, not ethnically Jewish, who as in previous good place fashion had observed the lives of the people of Israel, wanted that relationship with God, and so were following God's ways as demonstrated by the people of Israel.

Prior to the day of Pentecost, while Jesus was still on earth and many of the leaders of Israel were actively rejecting Him and His teaching, He told them a parable of a vineyard owner:

"Hear another parable. There was a master of a house who planted a vineyard and put a fence around it and dug a winepress in it and built a tower and leased it to tenants, and went into another country. When the season for fruit drew near, he sent his servants to the tenants to get his fruit. And the tenants took his servants and beat one, killed another, and stoned another. Again he sent other servants, more than the first. And they did the same to them. Finally he sent his son to them, saying, 'They will respect my son.' But when the tenants saw the son, they said to themselves, 'This is the heir. Come, let us kill him and have his inheritance.' And they took him and threw him out of the vineyard and killed him. When therefore the owner of the vineyard comes, what will he do to those tenants?" They said to him, "He will put those wretches to a miserable death and let out the vineyard to other tenants who will give him the fruits in their seasons."

Jesus said to them, "Have you never read in the Scriptures:

> "'The stone that the builders rejected
>   has become the cornerstone;
> this was the Lord's doing,
>   and it is marvelous in our eyes'?

Therefore I tell you, the kingdom of God will be taken away from you and given to a people producing its fruits." (Matthew 21:33–43; also see Mark 12:1–12; Luke 20:9–18)

We see God working through the people and nation of Israel, through their leaders' rejection of Jesus, to form a new "nation," one that has no national boundary.

Later, in Matthew 28:18–20 we read:

> And Jesus came and said to them, "All authority in heaven and on earth has been given to me. Go therefore and make disciples of all nations, baptizing them in the name of the Father and of the Son and of the Holy Spirit, teaching them to observe all that I have commanded you. And behold, I am with you always, to the end of the age."

This new form of God's work in the world to build up Good Places where we can live God's way and experience God's blessing does not introduce a break from God's work with the nation of Israel, but a continuation and an expansion of it.

This is emphasized earlier in Mathew 5:17–18, where Jesus said:

> Do not think that I have come to abolish the Law or the Prophets; I have not come to abolish them but to fulfill them. For truly, I say to you, until heaven and earth pass away, not an iota, not a dot, will pass from the Law until all is accomplished.

And in Matthew 13:52, we read:

> And he said to them, "Therefore every scribe who has been trained for the kingdom of heaven is like a master of a house, who brings out of his treasure what is new and what is old."

To all disciples of Jesus, regardless of nation, race, or ethnicity, the Bible takes the law that explains life as God intends and explains in many different ways how to love the Lord our God with all our hearts, with all our minds, and with all our strength, and to love our neighbors as ourselves, everywhere. We live to establish Good Places everywhere in which people live according to God's ways, His principles and values. And we accept the Good News that God's grace to live in a way that God will bless comes through the life, death, and resurrection of Jesus.

In the *middle*, the Bible continues to describe God's purpose, building a place that is good where we experience life as God intends, where we live life the way the Designer intends, where we experience His blessing, and where He is glorified. This was to occur in the Promised Land and Solomon's kingdom for the people of Israel and is extended beyond Israel to include every nation and every person who will follow Jesus and be the people of the Church. This is also what is meant by God's Kingdom—a place where Jesus is King, where His ways are being lived out, where we are filled with His joy, and where our joy is full. It is a place where Jesus and His principles and values are followed. In the New Testament, God's Kingdom resides in the hearts of individual people who believe in Jesus, and then collectively, in the body of Christ, the Church, a figurative Good Place. Contrary to popular opinion, the Church is not an event we attend or a building we go to. It is a people believing and following Jesus and living out life as God intends—a life and community of love and shalom.

In John 13:35, we read:

> By this all people will know that you are my disciples, if you have love for one another.

In Luke 10, Jesus sends out disciples to different towns, and no matter if that town accepted or rejected the disciples and their teaching, they were instructed to tell that town, "The Kingdom of God has come near you" (Luke 10:9 and 11). The people of these towns were being offered a way of life to follow Jesus and His ways, a life of love, shalom, flourishing, and blessing. Upon Jesus's departure from this earth, the Church is to take up that model and those characteristics and build a certain kind of community, a *Good Place.*

The Back

At the end of the Bible, we see the ultimate culmination of God's purpose, gifts, and calling, which will ultimately be achieved, coming together in perfect restoration. We read in Romans 11:29:

> For the gifts and the calling of God are irrevocable.

A little later in the same chapter, Paul, the author of Romans, exclaims:

> Oh, the depth of the riches and wisdom and knowledge of God! How unsearchable are his judgments and how inscrutable his ways!
>
> "For who has known the mind of the Lord,
>   or who has been his counselor?"
> "Or who has given a gift to him
>   that he might be repaid?"
>
> For from him and through him and to him are all things. To him be glory forever. Amen. (Romans 11:33–36)

In Revelation, the last book of the Bible, that culminating, perfectly restored place is described:

> Then I saw a new heaven and a new earth, for the first heaven and the first earth had passed away, and the sea was no more. And I saw the holy city, new Jerusalem, coming down out of heaven from God, prepared as a bride adorned for her husband. And I heard a loud voice from the throne saying, "Behold, the dwelling place of God is with man. He will dwell with them, and they will be his people, and God himself will be with them as their God. He will wipe away every tear from their eyes, and death shall be no more, neither shall there be mourning, nor crying, nor pain anymore, for the former things have passed away." (Revelation 21:1–4)

> And I saw no temple in the city, for its temple is the Lord God the Almighty and the Lamb. And the city has no need of sun or moon to shine on it, for the glory of God gives it light, and its lamp is the Lamb. By its light will the nations walk, and the kings of the earth will bring their glory into it, and its gates will never be shut by day—and there will be no night there. They will bring into it the glory and the honor of the nations. But nothing unclean will ever enter it, nor anyone who does what is detestable or false, but only those who are written in the Lamb's book of life. (Revelation 21:22–27)

> Then the angel showed me the river of the water of life, bright as crystal, flowing from the throne of God and of the Lamb through the middle of the street of the city; also, on either side of the river, the tree of life with its twelve kinds of fruit, yielding its fruit each month. The leaves of the tree were for the healing of the nations. No longer will there be anything accursed, but the throne of God and of the Lamb will be in it, and his servants will worship him. They will see his face, and his name will be on their foreheads. And night will be no more. They will need no light of lamp or sun, for the Lord God will be their light, and they will reign forever and ever. (Revelation 22:1–5)

At the *back* of the Bible, in the Book of Revelation, it describes a "new heaven and new earth." It is interesting to note that this new place is here on earth and not in some far-off, ethereal place we are completely unfamiliar with. We were created and designed to live on earth. This is a place where all things are made new, with original purpose and intention, where life as God intends it will be perfected; where people will experience perfect love, joy, and shalom; where we will perfectly image and reflect the characteristics of the One who created us. This is not just a *Good Place*, it is a *Perfect Place*, and we have an opportunity to enjoy God and it perfectly forever!

CHAPTER 6

A BRIEF STORYLINE OF THE GOOD NEWS
OF THE BIBLE

I n this chapter, we will walk through the four-part storyline of the Good News of the Bible with an overarching and descriptive theme of *shalom* and directly relate the storyline to work, organizational life, and life in a Good Place. For more on the concept of a four-part gospel, we refer you to Hugh Welchel's book entitled *How Then Should We Work*.[5]

CREATION

In the beginning, God created *ex nihilo*, out of nothing (Genesis 1:1; Hebrews 11:3). He created the heavens and the earth, light, water, land, vegetation, animals, living creatures, and human beings. At the end of each day of creating, God said what He had created was "good" (Genesis 1:10, 12, 18, 21, 25). Just after He created people, when His original creation was finished, He said it was "very good" (Genesis 1:31).

---

5   Hugh Welchel, *How Then Should We Work* (Bloomington, IN: WestBow Press, 2012), 8-13.

Good

Very Good

When we read the creation account in the Book of Genesis and reflections of it throughout the Bible, and for our context of organizational life, we notice themes and characteristics that God creates and that were good and very good.

We read that God created human beings in His image and to image Him in and to the world (Genesis 1:26–28). Among other attributes, this automatically and inherently gives every human being purpose, worth, value, dignity, and identity, unlike anything else in all creation. His image means we were created to be relational because He is relational. We were meant to have relationship with Him and with each other. His image means we were created to be creative because He is Creator and creative. We have the opportunity to co-create with Him and continue His creation in a way that continues to enhance and build upon that which was originally created (Genesis 1:26–28; 2:15). In much the same way, we were created to work because He is a worker and is constantly at work. We have opportunity to work with God's creation (the natural world, the earth, raw materials, etc.). The work we do has meaning and should be fulfilling in a way that builds up and is life-giving. He commands us to work in this way. We image Him in many other ways; these are just a few for our context.

We read that God created a place to live and work. God made a place where we had everything we needed, where we could live in a way that He intends, He could bless us, His majesty would be on display, and He would be glorified; a place of love, peace, wholeness, flourishing, well-being, joy, and beauty. The people God created walked and talked with God, unencumbered, fully known, and fully loved by God and each other. A way to ultimately describe this place and their experience is the word *shalom*, meaning they had perfect and harmonious relationship with God, with each other, and with the rest of creation.

SHALOM

We then read that God commanded the people to do things, telling them to "be fruitful and multiply and fill the earth and subdue it" (Genesis 1:28), calling them to populate the world with people, image bearers, creating culture and society, working and stewarding creation. This is commonly known as the Cultural Mandate and is closely related to the Great Commission, where later in the Bible, in the New Testament Book of Matthew, Jesus told His disciples, "Go therefore and make disciples of all nations, baptizing them in the name of the Father and of the Son and of the Holy Spirit, teaching them to observe all that I have commanded you" (Matthew 28:19–20a). A commission and command to go and multiply, filling the earth with disciples, people who bear God's image, who follow Him, who glorify Him, and who enjoy His shalom.

We also read that God put the people in the garden "to work it and keep it" (Genesis 2:15) and gave them dominion over living creatures and plants for food, to steward that which He created. God created work and it was good. Work was something we were designed to do as image bearers and partners with God in His work in the world. God is a worker, and He is always at work (John 5:17). Our work in this world was intended to be meaningful, fulfilling, and a way we develop ourselves and the creation around us. There was no distinction between "sacred" work and "non-sacred" work. All of life and work was (and is) sacred as it was purposed, and we were designed by God to engage in it to His glory and our shalom. We are co-creators with God in a sense, with the opportunity to experience the continuing of creation in us and through our activities. *A Good Place.*

2

THE PROBLEM

We certainly do not experience this kind of place in the current world we live in. What happened? We, God's created people, decided we did not want to believe God, follow His design, or live the way He intends for us to live (Genesis 3). God told the people He created that they could enjoy and take in everything in the garden, except for one thing (Genesis 2:16–17). You can have full access to all of that which has been created for you to flourish and thrive, only do not do one thing. If you are a human being, you get this dilemma. When someone tells you that you can do whatever you want within this space except one thing, what do you want to do? When you were a child visiting your grandparents' house and Grandma said you can go into any room except that one, which room did you want to explore first? That's right. You and I want to do that one thing we are told not to do. At this point in human history, Adam and Eve did the same thing. Instead of believing (and having faith in) God and His Word, they decided to believe the Deceiver, who said in short, "Did God actually say…?" (Genesis 3:1). The Deceiver asked this question and caused other questions to arise and challenge God's Word and His ways. Questions like: Does God *really* have your best interest in mind? Is God trying to keep something good from you? Are God's ways *really* better? If you do this thing, then your eyes will be open and you will be like God, knowing and taking in good and evil (Genesis 3:5). We succumbed to the lies of the Deceiver, believed that lie, did not believe God, and as a result acted out of that unbelief. This line of thinking and action is known as "sin." This was the "original sin." It is the original sin that entered the world through the original people. It is the lie we still believe and the sin that still affects us today.

At this time in history, where the concept and problem of human sin is introduced, let us pause and consider the answer to the question: "What is sin?" The Bible defines sin in Romans 14:23b simply as "whatever does not proceed from faith." The Bible says that faith is the assurance of things we hope for and the conviction of things we cannot see (Hebrews 11:1), meaning we think, behave, and operate out of a motivation of our trust, confidence, and belief in God, who He is and what He does, even though we have not seen Him personally. The Bible goes on to say that it is impossible to please God without faith (Hebrews 11:6). Another description is that all sin is, or stems from, unbelief—an unbelief about God, about who He is and His character, what He did and continues to do. Adam and Eve did not act in faith as they believed the Deceiver and acted on their own judgment rather than believing God and His Word. They acted out of that unbelief, as they did not believe the truth about God but believed a lie about who He is, what He said, what He was doing—and, therefore, a lie about who we are as created people made in His image.

Sin may be distilled down to one word: *pride*. We may even go as far as to say that pride is the only sin. What is pride? Pride can be defined as a feeling that you are more important or better than other people,[6] that you are superior. Pride gives you an excessively high view of yourself, and in this case, you have your best interest in mind and you know what is best for you. Not the Creator. Not the Designer. You. You define what is best. You define what success is. Therefore, we can define pride as thinking, believing, and acting as if we know better than God, and therefore, we act like our own god. One might suggest that all the man-made problems of the world stem from this simple, yet difficult, concept. We want to be God. We think that we are that important. The Bible says there is one God. And guess what, we are not Him. I do not think it is a coincidence that this is also the first Commandment found in the Ten Commandments, "I am the Lord your God … You shall have no other gods before me" (Exodus 20:2–3). It's hard to get

---

6   *Merriam-Webster*, s.v. "pride," accessed September 1, 2021, https://www.merriam-webster.com/dictionary/pride.

through to breaking the other commandments without breaking the first one. This was certainly the dilemma Adam and Eve experienced, and may I say, we have experienced it throughout history and still do every day.

So what were and are the consequences of this problem of sin—this unbelief, pride, and operating without faith? What is wrong with the world? A simple yet eternally catastrophic answer is "dis-shalom." This is not a real word, but it describes what we lost when sin entered the world and the consequences the original humans experienced, and we still experience today. We now experience the opposite of shalom, meaning we experience broken harmony and relationship with God, with each other, and with creation.

The Bible says that because we operate without faith, we are alienated, estranged, separated, and even hostile in our minds toward God (Colossians 1:21). We also experience dysfunctional relationships (that is very much an understatement in many cases) with each other in many and various forms through things like thinking more highly of ourselves than we ought, unloving actions, disunity, racism, injustice, murder, human trafficking, etc. Lastly, we experience a creation that, as the Bible says, "is groaning" (Romans 8:22) through things like tornadoes, droughts, hurricanes, earthquakes, pollution, and famine. We have not come across anyone who can disagree with this simple, yet extremely profound, truth about the human condition in these three spheres when describing our current experience or throughout human history. We all can agree that the world and humanity have a problem.

DIS-SHALOM

In the context of work, this problem and the consequence of "dis-shalom" have a very real application. As we stated, one of the consequences of sin is that we lost our harmony or harmonious relationship with creation. One of those things that was created for us was work. Therefore, we also lost our harmonious relationship with meaningful, fulfilling, life-developing work. Now the ground is cursed (Genesis 3:17). We can imagine rocks, weeds, and hard clay appearing in the once fertile soil that was so easily cultivated. The sun became very hot. Work became really hard, frustrating, toilsome, painful, and sweaty. Unfortunately, that is what a vast majority of workers have experienced since then and today. Then the purpose for work becomes less about something that is fulfilling and meaningful, something we were designed to do that makes us and the world around us better, and it turns into something else—some good, some not. On one end of the spectrum, it turns work into something meaningless where it is just a means to an end. Some of those ends are good, such as providing for ourselves and our family. Some are not so good, like simply a way to make money so we can buy and do what we want when we are not working—on the weekend or after retirement. On this end, think of how we consciously or unconsciously perpetuate this idea of working for the weekend, or working and saving enough to retire so we can finally do what we really want to do. Or on the opposite end of the spectrum, work becomes too meaningful, to the point that the work we do becomes who we are, where we find our value, our worth, and our identity. On this end, think of how we consciously or unconsciously perpetuate this concept. Think of the second question you ask someone after meeting them and getting to know their name. More often than not, the next questions are: "What do you do?" or "Where do you work?" Then we automatically put that person in a category of their value, how we interact with them, if we are impressed or not, etc. Just for fun, after you learn a new person's name, try making the second question, "Who are you?" and see what kind of response you get.

According to the Bible, God is love, grace, mercy, blessing, and all those wonderful things that we like about God. The Bible also describes God as just, truth, righteous, and holy. Sometimes these are attributes we think we don't like about God. But nonetheless, these are real attributes of God, and He is perfect in all of them. When we do not believe God and the truth about His character, and thus do not live life according to His ways, we ultimately decide to not do life the way He designed and intends (for His glory and for our optimal joy). The result is that we cannot be in the presence of a perfectly holy, righteous, loving, and just God. The decision to not believe God or follow His ways has destructive temporal consequences and dire eternal consequences of continuing this separation and broken relationship with God, each other, and His creation forever if we do not find a solution to fix it.

When we believe and act this way, meaning we do not want to "hang out" with God and follow His ways now, why would He think we want to "hang out" with Him and follow His ways for all of eternity? That's what heaven is—eternity with God is being with Him, believing and loving Him, and living life the way He intends, where He receives glory and we are blessed with unsurpassed joy and shalom.

In general, we cannot think of anyone on our planet earth who would not say that we, that is humanity, have a problem. Certainly no one would say we live in an ideal state of things where we are in complete, harmonious relationship with God, each other, and creation. We may disagree on what the problem is, or some may describe it differently than we just did, but we can generally agree that there is a problem in the world where we live in dysfunction between us and God, between us as humans, and between us and the creation. God hates this state of dis-shalom that is the present human condition and experience. It is not the way He originally created and designed things.

2

THE PROBLEM

DIS-SHALOM

Work
Not Good!

3

THE SOLUTION

In the stating of a solution to our human and world problem, there is an ideal to be reached. To solve our problem and reach the ideal, there generally exists two worldviews, two basic approaches. To illustrate each of these worldviews, we can imagine humanity at the bottom of a ladder (or a mountain if you prefer) and the ideal state at the top. The solution needs to get us from our problem state to the ideal state and provide the method or means to get us from where we are to where we want to be.

The first worldview is where we can look to ourselves for the solution to fix the problem. We can see this worldview through either a secular or a religious lens. We simply look to ourselves, our own intelligence, ingenuity, experiences, education, and how much smarter and more enlightened we are than those before us. Or we "work together with god" to help us achieve this ideal. This is the general worldview purported by atheists, humanists, other deists, and non-Christian views of the world. This may even be the most popular worldview that exists in our day. It basically says that it is up to us (or us with god) to do better, get better, strive to be better and better, that we just have to do and be "gooder" and "gooder" to ascend to the ideal so that we can eventually reach the ideal pinnacle at the top of the ladder, or the mountain, that we all are climbing and is being espoused by this first worldview. This assumes human goodness and perfection is somehow within our control if we just have enough time, if there are enough smart people in the room to figure it out, and if we can all agree on what the better or ideal standard we are aspiring to is.

IDEAL

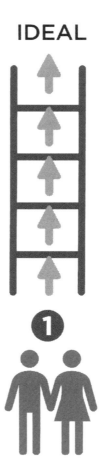

Unfortunately, therein lies one of the problems. In this worldview, the ideal, or the standard of what is good, is either never defined or, worse yet, changes with culture and, therefore, not everyone agrees on what it is. How would we feel if we were striving to be good enough but we never knew how good enough we had to be, or it kept changing? The other issue with this worldview is that we know that we can never be good enough to reach this ideal. All this sounds more than a little discouraging, even overwhelming and impossible.

Fortunately for us, there exists a second worldview. In this worldview, the ideal is defined. It is defined in the Bible as complete holiness and righteousness. It could simply be called perfection. On the surface, this can also sound very discouraging and impossible because we all know we cannot be perfect. No matter how smart we are or how good we try to be, we will never be perfect. The Bible actually talks about this in Romans 3:23, where it says that "all have sinned and fall short of the glory of God." This sounds very discouraging and defeating—unless the solution does not come from within us but comes from outside us and the world.

In the second worldview, only espoused in the Bible, perfection is not something you work for, ascend to, earn, or can achieve by any performance or work you do. Perfection is something available and given to you because of God's great love and grace toward His creation. The solution of the ideal, or perfection, in this worldview is a gift. It is a gift we receive by faith and is not something we work for or earn or can ever be good enough to acquire or deserve. It is simply something we believe and accept (Ephesians 2:8–9). The standard bar is set at holiness (Leviticus 20:26; 1 Peter 1:15–16) and perfection (Matthew 5:48). The Good News, then, is that the Author who defines the good and perfect standard also provides the solution to achieving the standard. Instead of us ascending to this perfection, perfection descends and comes to us as a gift allowing us to be viewed as perfect by God even though we do not act perfectly. This is a mystery of this Good News. Perfection is a gift, and the gift has a name. His name is Jesus, the Author and Perfector of the Christian faith (Hebrews 12:2). The solution to our problem is Jesus (God who came to earth in human form) and His gift of perfection, where He substitutes His perfection for our imperfection, His righteousness and holiness for our falling short in these areas. The result is a changed heart and a transformed mind, a heart of love and a life of shalom. This is the Christian worldview according to the Bible and is the one thing that makes Christianity different from every other worldview.

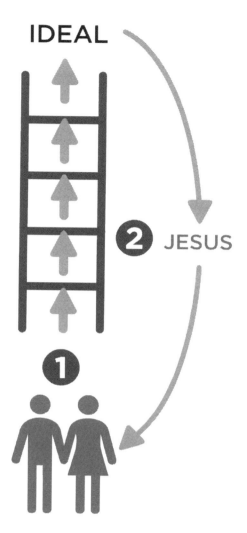

IDEAL

2 JESUS

1

The Bible says that we could never be good enough, holy enough, or righteous enough to live up to the ideal standard of perfection that it takes to have harmonious relationship with God now and forever. God's justice will not allow it; however, His grace provides the solution for it. So God, through His Son Jesus and in His love, mercy, and grace, does for us what we cannot do for ourselves. He came to earth to live the life we could not live, die the death we should have died (as the just consequence of our sin), satisfy the justice that we should be satisfying, and defeat the power of death by resurrecting from the grave. He provides a way for us to be redeemed from our problem, where we can have our broken relationship with God, with each other, and with creation mended. He provides a way for us to be perfect when we could not do perfect on our own.

Why does God do this? The Bible says because He loves us (John 3:16) and He desires us to glorify Him (1 Corinthians 10:31) and have optimal joy (John 15:11) and enjoy an abundant, fulfilling life (John 10:10). He desires that we would have hearts of love and lives of shalom both now (although only in a partial sense) and into eternity (perfectly and fully). This is the essence of the Lord's Prayer (Matthew 6:9–13), where Jesus teaches us to pray that His Kingdom will come and His will be done on earth as it is in heaven. His Kingdom is a place where He is King, where we live life the way He intends it, a life of shalom—peace, harmony, completeness, richness, well-being, wholeness—giving thanks and glorifying the Author of creation, the Architect of the universe, and the Designer of life. This is the essence of the Great Commandment to love God and love people, and the Great Commission to make disciples.

Have you ever received the perfect gift? Someone who knew you really well gave you a wonderful gift for your birthday, let's say. You receive the gift and open it. You look at it for the first time. Your eyes open wide. Your mouth drops open. You hold it up gazing at it for a moment to admire its beautiful features and reflect briefly on the love that motivated the gift giver. You move it to the side and make eye contact with the person who gave you this wonderful and perfect gift. Maybe you even get up, walk over, give them a hug, but most assuredly you say, "Thank you!" This is a picture of us, the solution to our problems, and our life thereafter. We can receive God's gift of perfection, gaze upon its beauty, love, and grace, and then we say "thank you" with the rest of our lives, living in a constant state of acknowledgment and thanksgiving to the ultimate gift Giver, imaging more of God and becoming more like Jesus.

When and if we do this, please know it does not mean that life is suddenly comfortable, easy, and full of all of the pleasures we could ever imagine. But what it does mean, as we have previously discussed, is we have the opportunity to live with a heart of love and a life of shalom.

In the book *Into the Depths of God*,[7] Calvin Miller draws the analogy between snorkeling and scuba diving. So I like to call this life experience "scuba diving shalom." In snorkeling, we are completely in the water enjoying the beauty beneath the ocean from a position of floating on the surface. In scuba diving, we are completely submerged into the depth of the ocean where we are able to enjoy its beauty up close and personal. If you are snorkeling and waves or a storm comes, what do you experience? Yes, you experience being tossed by the waves and the storm. If you are scuba diving, what do you experience when those same waves or storm comes? The answer is that you are so submerged into the calmness and peace of the ocean depths and so up close and personal to its beauty that the situation on the surface has little to no impact on your experience. It does not mean the waves and the storm do not happen, as the Bible tells us, even promises, they surely will. It means that when they occur, we never cease to experience God's love (Romans 8:35–39) and shalom, and we can then operate out of that love and shalom.

In the context of work and organizational life, there is also an opportunity for a solution, to redeem and recapture the goodness of work we lost, to transform our work and workplaces into something that reflects God's intent and the Biblical purpose for work. Work was and is meant to be a meaningful and to fulfill God's call on our lives—something people were designed to do. Work can be a spiritual, sacred act that positively impacts individual lives and makes the world a better place, allowing more and more people to experience life the way God intends it to be. Work and organizational life has an opportunity to be a transformative place where we are building up hearts of love and lives of shalom.

---

7   Calvin Miller, *Into the Depths of God: Where Eyes See the Invisible, Ears Hear the Inaudible, and Minds Conceive the Inconceivable* (Bloomington, MN: Bethany House, 2001).

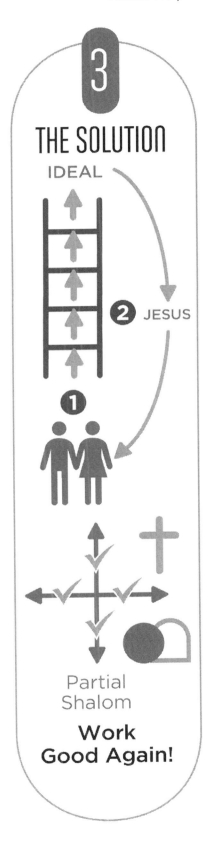

Having walked through the storyline to this point, we know and experience that we live in the problem and the solution, and through Jesus's perfect substitution and righteous atonement for those who believe in Him, we can experience this redemption and shalom only partially now. However, and thankfully, the Good News of the Bible and Jesus's Gospel does not end here.

4

PERFECTION

In the Book of John, Jesus shares with His disciples, and all believers, that He is going to prepare a place for us, and He will come again and will take us to Himself, that where He is, there we may be also (John 14:3). Later, in the final book of the Bible, this same author, John, shares the following:

> Then I saw a new heaven and a new earth, for the first heaven and the first earth had passed away, and the sea was no more. And I saw the holy city, new Jerusalem, coming down out of heaven from God, prepared as a bride adorned for her husband. And I heard a loud voice from the throne saying, "Behold, the dwelling place of God is with man. He will dwell with them, and they will be his people, and God himself will be with them as their God. He will wipe away every tear from their eyes, and death shall be no more, neither shall there be mourning, nor crying, nor pain anymore, for the former things have passed away."

> And he who was seated on the throne said, "Behold, I am making all things new." Also he said, "Write this down, for these words are trustworthy and true." (Revelation 21:1–5)

In this part of the story, we move from having the opportunity to experience this shalom partially and imperfectly, to experiencing shalom fully and perfectly, in a perfect place, where God Himself will reside with us. Right now we are experiencing the "not yet," but we will experience this "to be" when Jesus returns and establishes His Kingdom on earth, where He will reign as King forever, and where we get to "hang out" with Him forever. This will no longer be a Good Place strived for, but a perfect place fully restored and fully experienced. This will be a place where we live in perfect shalom, perfect harmonious relationship with God, with each other, and with this new creation. People will experience perfectly restored peace, completeness, richness, well-being, and wholeness. We will perfectly live out the purpose for which we were created, to glorify God and enjoy Him forever, in the ways He designed us to live.

And many believe work will be a significant part of what we do. We will continue to work, only it will be fully restored to its intended meaning and fulfillment, allowing us to continue to co-create with the Creator, bringing Him much glory and bringing us much joy. We will experience all of this for eternity with Him in a perfect place.

PERFECTION

JESUS

All Things New

Perfect Place

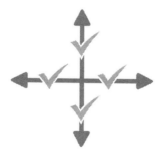

Complete
and
Fulfilled Shalom

Work
Perfect!

And, if we put the story together, we have a brief storyline of the Gospel, the Good News as told in the Bible:

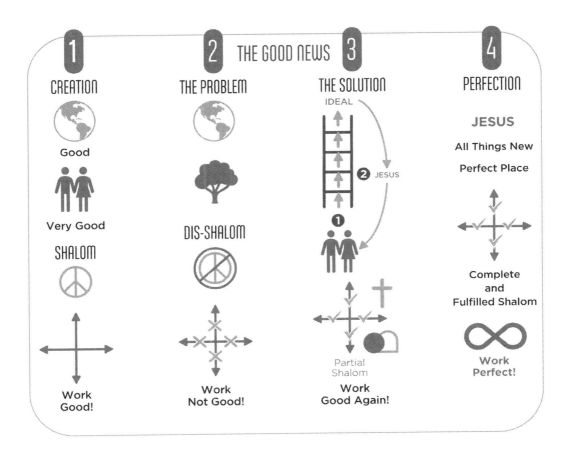

CHAPTER 7

THE SACRED-SECULAR MYTH

I n order to understand the sacred-secular myth, let us first define our terms. *Sacred* is defined as something dedicated or set apart for the service or worship of a deity, worthy of religious veneration (reverence, admiration, etc.).[8] *Secular*, on the other hand, is defined as something of or relating to the worldly or temporal, not overtly or specifically religious.[9] The idea then is that there exists a divide between that which is sacred and that which is secular.

The roots of this sacred-secular divide go all the way back to some of the early philosophers and church fathers. For instance, Aristotle taught that it was demeaning to do work with your hands or work for pay.[10] Augustine separated life into the active and the contemplative. Both the active and contemplative lives were good, but the contemplative was of a higher order. Martin Luther's Reformation attempted to recapture the Biblical view of work, where work is meaningful, fulfills God's call on our lives, and is something people were designed to do, as well as restore the belief that work itself can be a spiritual and sacred act. In the Enlightenment period, philosophers like Immanuel Kant once again separated the world into two categories: fact and reason, or moral and spiritual.[11] Unfortunately, this divided thinking infiltrated the church and influences our thinking even today.

Simply stated, the sacred-secular divide is where we treat things as an either/or proposition: either sacred or secular. For instance, we may have learned to treat as sacred or secular the immaterial versus material world, one day versus another day, church roles and activities versus marketplace roles and activities. More specifically, we may think the work or the vocations of a pastor, priest, missionary, Bible teacher, or the like are somehow more sacred than work or vocations such as being an engineer, accountant, police officer, cashier, student, athlete, teacher, or business leader. We may have learned that these secular roles or activities are at best just "platforms to share our faith" or are simply there to provide the means to support the truly sacred work. We may have learned that in order to make these secular activities pleasing or more glorifying to God, we need to sprinkle in some sacred activities into them, like figuring out how to pray or have a Bible study during these secular activities.

---

8   *Merriam-Webster, s.v. "sacred,"* accessed September 1, 2021, https://www.merriam-webster.com/dictionary/sacred.

9   *Merriam-Webster, s.v. "secular,"* accessed September 1, 2021, https://www.merriam-webster.com/dictionary/secular.

10   Hugh Welchel, *How Then Should We Work* (Bloomington, IN: Westbow Press, 2012), 57.

11   Hugh Welchel, *"The Historical Influences of the Sacred-Secular Divide," Institute for Faith, Work & Economics* (October 17, 2016), https://tifwe.org/historical-influences-of-the-sacred-secular-divide.

We definitely should be good Christians while engaging in these secular activities, being honest, kind, ethical, hard-working people. But most of us have been taught that these "secular" activities are not really sacred activities on par with praying or reading the Bible.

The activities or roles that have been traditionally viewed as sacred are good things for sure, but referring to them as the *only* sacred things is significantly lacking in the full purpose of life and, specifically, work as designed and intended by the Author and Creator (as we learned in the previous sections of this book and will discuss in the next section on The Purpose of Work). The Bible teaches a more holistic view of the sacred. All things are sacred and have divine meaning and purpose. All things can please and bring glory to God in and of themselves when viewed as a means of grace, acknowledging the Author of all things, giving thanks to God, being motivated out of a heart of love for Him, engaging with a view that this is an opportunity to co-create with the Creator, to enhance that which God has given to us to continue His creation, to develop, cultivate, steward, enhance that which He originally created. God receives glory when we steward His creation in a way that makes us better (reaching our full God-given potential in the activity and in becoming more like Him), makes those around us and the community better (having an opportunity to experience life the way God intends it), makes the object of our work better (cultivating, developing, innovating it), and makes the world better (bringing His Kingdom and His ways of operating in that Kingdom here on earth).

In the context of this book, our work and organizational life was and is designed and intended to be much more than the secular view we have come to learn. Not so much more that it becomes our identity, which so many in our culture have done, and not so much less (the "secular view") that it does not possess its intended sacred meaning and purpose. When work has its rightful place in our lives as a part of what we were created and designed to do, and simply doing it well, imaging God in it, allowing it to mold, shape, and develop us; giving us opportunities to love, serve, and care for others; making the world look more like the Kingdom; and thankfully acknowledging the Author for work as a means of grace, it brings God glory and fulfills His purposes for us and in the world.

Acts 17:28 says, "In him [God], we live and move and have our being…" Our identity and all we do is meaningfully and deeply connected to God. Ephesians 4:6 states that there is "one God and Father of all, who is over all and through all and in all." Evidently, in these Bible passages the author intended the word "all" for a purpose. The Bible also says in John 17:15 that "I do not ask that you take them out of the world, but that you keep them from the evil one." We are to live in the world, stay engaged in the world, and no matter what vocation we are called to, our mission is the same: to image God, making Him look great by all we do and creating places for people to experience the characteristics of Him and His Kingdom.

The sacred-secular divide, according to the Bible, is a myth at best, and an untruth at worst. According to the Bible, all things are sacred. All things have meaning to God. All things are to be done in light of and through faith in God. This gets us back to the earlier described storyline of the Bible where we saw that sin is anything done without faith (Romans 14:23) and without faith it is impossible to please God (Hebrews 11:6). So, we live, move, and have our being in God (Acts 17:28), and this pleases Him and is a part of our purpose for being.

In short, and for our organizational context, we believe the Bible teaches that work is sacred and is a "means of grace" created by God, something human beings were designed to do, something that God calls us to, and something that brings meaning and fulfillment, with the intent that our work makes us better, those around us better, our organization better, our industry better, our community better, and the world a better place where we build up hearts of love and lives of shalom. Work gives us an opportunity to fulfill parts of our design, a means to change us and develop us into our God-given potential, an opportunity to image God, the original Creator and ongoing Worker, an opportunity to become more like Jesus, the perfect embodiment of God's image, an opportunity to use our gifts in service to a greater good, ultimately glorifying God and bringing shalom to ourselves and the world around us.

CHAPTER 8

THE PURPOSE OF WORK

Let's start with a few foundational questions about work: *Where did work begin? Why do we work? What is the purpose of work in a Good Place?*

To answer these questions, we travel back to the beginning of human history, to the story of creation in the Book of Genesis. We have already discussed these beginnings in the *Front, Middle, Back,* and again in chapter 4, "A Brief Storyline of the Good News of the Bible." As we dive a little further into the actual text, we find our principles and values about work.[12] These excerpts from Genesis 1 through 3 give us a quick synopsis that will help to begin to answer these questions:

> In the beginning, God created the heavens and the earth…
> And God said, "Let there be light," and there was light…
> And God said, "Let there be an expanse in the midst of the waters, and let it separate the waters from the waters."…
> And God said, "Let the waters under the heavens be gathered together into one place, and let the dry land appear."…
> And God saw that it was good.
>
> And God said, "Let the earth sprout vegetation, plants yielding seed, and fruit trees bearing fruit in which is their seed, each according to its kind, on the earth."…
> And God saw that it was good.
>
> And God said, "Let there be lights in the expanse of the heavens to separate the day from the night. And let them be for signs and for seasons, and for days and years, and let them be lights in the expanse of the heavens to give light upon the earth."…
> And God saw that it was good.
>
> And God said, "Let the waters swarm with swarms of living creatures, and let birds fly above the earth across the expanse of the heavens."… And God blessed them, saying, "Be fruitful and multiply and fill the waters in the seas, and let birds multiply on the earth."…
> And God said, "Let the earth bring forth living creatures according to their kinds—livestock and creeping things and beasts of the earth according to their kinds."…
> And God saw that it was good.

---

12   Scott Myers, *Finding Value: The Art of Life in Organizations* (Akron, OH: Eutopia Report, Inc., 2005).

Then God said, "Let us make man in our image, after our likeness. And let them have dominion over the fish of the sea and over the birds of the heavens and over the livestock and over all the earth and over every creeping thing that creeps on the earth."

So God created man in his own image,
in the image of God he created him;
male and female he created them.

And God blessed them. And God said to them, "Be fruitful and multiply and fill the earth and subdue it, and have dominion over the fish of the sea and over the birds of the heavens and over every living thing that moves on the earth." And God said, "Behold, I have given you every plant yielding seed that is on the face of all the earth, and every tree with seed in its fruit. You shall have them for food. And to every beast of the earth and to every bird of the heavens and to everything that creeps on the earth, everything that has the breath of life, I have given every green plant for food." And it was so. And God saw everything that he had made, and behold, it was very good…

And the Lord God planted a garden in Eden, in the east, and there he put the man whom he had formed. And out of the ground the Lord God made to spring up every tree that is pleasant to the sight and good for food. The tree of life was in the midst of the garden, and the tree of the knowledge of good and evil…

The Lord God took the man and put him in the garden of Eden to work it and keep it. And the Lord God commanded the man, saying, "You may surely eat of every tree of the garden, but of the tree of the knowledge of good and evil you shall not eat…"

And to Adam he said,
"Because you have listened to the voice of your wife
    and have eaten of the tree
of which I commanded you,
    'You shall not eat of it,'
cursed is the ground because of you;
    in pain you shall eat of it all the days of your life;
thorns and thistles it shall bring forth for you;
    and you shall eat the plants of the field.
By the sweat of your face
    you shall eat bread,
till you return to the ground,
    for out of it you were taken;
for you are dust,
    and to dust you shall return." (Genesis 1:1, 3, 6, 9–12, 14–15, 18, 20, 22, 24–31; 2:8–9, 15–17; 3:17–19)

In the beginning, God created, and what He created was good and very good. As illustrated by these excerpts from the story of creation, one of the things He created was work, and it was good. Work is often an overlooked aspect of God's good creation. Work was fulfilling, meaningful, and purposeful. The work was to be fruitful and multiply, to fill the earth and subdue it, to grow the population and build society and culture. It was to work and care for the garden, to cultivate, farm, tend, guard, and keep it. It was to have dominion, to rule over, to manage, and to be responsible for the living creatures in a way that cares for God's creation. This is commonly referred to as the Cultural Mandate (and is closely related to the Great Commission found in the Book of Matthew in the New Testament of the Bible). Ultimately, we were called to steward that which God has entrusted to the people He created. We are to be trustees of God's estate and everything in it. We are also called to co-create along with God, continuing to "create" and develop that which He originally created, to enhance and develop His creation, and return good things from His investment. Work, as originally designed, provided a means to do just what we were called and designed to do. Work is a means of grace.

There is another way to look at this creation story and derive meaning and purpose from work. In Genesis 1:27, we read:

> So God created man in his own image,
>   in the image of God he created him;
>   male and female he created them.

As we can see from this creation account, God is a worker and, in the beginning of history, His work was creating. To this day, God continues to work. He works in us and through us to fulfill His good purposes (Philippians 2:13). Therefore, if we are made in God's image and one of those image attributes is that God works and is a worker, part of us imaging Him is to work and be a worker to fulfill His good purposes in us and through us in the world.

What else does the Bible have to say about work?

The Bible refers to work hundreds of times throughout its pages, and our call to work is woven throughout the entire narrative of the Bible. In addition to the account in Genesis, here are several verses that further help inform and define the why, what, and how of work in Good Place organizations:

> For my thoughts are not your thoughts,
>   neither are your ways my ways, declares the LORD.
> For as the heavens are higher than the earth,
>   so are my ways higher than your ways
>   and my thoughts than your thoughts. (Isaiah 55:8–9)

> Whatever you do, work heartily, as for the Lord and not for men, 24 knowing that from the Lord you will receive the inheritance as your reward. You are serving the Lord Christ. (Colossians 3:23–24)

> See, I have called by name Bezalel the son of Uri, son of Hur, of the tribe of Judah, and I have filled him with the Spirit of God, with ability and

intelligence, with knowledge and all craftsmanship, to devise artistic designs, to work in gold, silver, and bronze, in cutting stones for setting, and in carving wood, to work in every craft. (Exodus 31:2–5)

Remember the Sabbath day, to keep it holy. Six days you shall labor, and do all your work, but the seventh day is a Sabbath to the Lord your God. On it you shall not do any work, you, or your son, or your daughter, your male servant, or your female servant, or your livestock, or the sojourner who is within your gates. For in six days the Lord made heaven and earth, the sea, and all that is in them, and rested on the seventh day. Therefore, the Lord blessed the Sabbath day and made it holy. (Exodus 20:8–11)

Now concerning brotherly love you have no need for anyone to write to you, for you yourselves have been taught by God to love one another, for that indeed is what you are doing to all the brothers throughout Macedonia. But we urge you, brothers, to do this more and more, and to aspire to live quietly, and to mind your own affairs, and to work with your hands, as we instructed you, so that you may walk properly before outsiders and be dependent on no one. (1 Thessalonians 4:9–12)

Therefore, my beloved brothers, be steadfast, immovable, always abounding in the work of the Lord, knowing that in the Lord your labor is not in vain. (1 Corinthians 15:58)

For you remember, brothers, our labor and toil: we worked night and day, that we might not be a burden to any of you, while we proclaimed to you the gospel of God. You are witnesses, and God also, how holy and righteous and blameless was our conduct toward you believers. For you know how, like a father with his children, we exhorted each one of you and encouraged you and charged you to walk in a manner worthy of God, who calls you into his own kingdom and glory. (1 Thessalonians 2:9–12)

For even when we were with you, we would give you this command: If anyone is not willing to work, let him not eat. (2 Thessalonians 3:10)

Do not be anxious about anything, but in everything by prayer and supplication with thanksgiving let your requests be made known to God. (Philippians 4:6)

Where there is no guidance, a people falls, but in an abundance of counselors there is safety. (Proverbs 11:14)

In all toil there is profit, but mere talk tends only to poverty. (Proverbs 14:23)

By wisdom a house is built, and by understanding it is established; by knowledge the rooms are filled with all precious and pleasant riches. (Proverbs 24:3–4)

Woe to him who builds a town with blood and founds a city on iniquity! Behold, is it not from the Lord of hosts that peoples labor merely for fire, and nations weary themselves for nothing? For the earth will be filled with the knowledge of the glory of the Lord as the waters cover the sea. (Habakkuk 2:12–14)

For his invisible attributes, namely, his eternal power and divine nature, have been clearly perceived, ever since the creation of the world, in the things that have been made. So they are without excuse. (Romans 1:20)

And if the ear should say, "Because I am not an eye, I do not belong to the body," that would not make it any less a part of the body. If the whole body were an eye, where would be the sense of hearing? If the whole body were an ear, where would be the sense of smell? But as it is, God arranged the members in the body, each one of them, as he chose. (1 Corinthians 12:16–18)

Come to me, all who labor and are heavy laden, and I will give you rest. Take my yoke upon you, and learn from me, for I am gentle and lowly in heart, and you will find rest for your souls. For my yoke is easy, and my burden is light. (Matthew 11:28–30)

So, whether you eat or drink, or whatever you do, do all to the glory of God. (1 Corinthians 10:31)

Certainly, there are many more verses we could look to about work. These selected verses are an attempt to capture the overall value and derive principles about work. For instance, God's thoughts on things, including work, are higher than our own thoughts. We are to work diligently, heartily, with excellence, and for the Lord. Work and rest are rhythmic themes throughout creation and in our work. God not only designed us to work, but He also has gifted us to do different, specialized work. We are to live and work quietly in a way that is not a burden to each other. We can work as an organized body to compliment and work for and with each other in a way that is more efficient, more effective, accomplishing more together than we could on our own. Our work provides for ourselves, our families, and others. Work allows us to live and have a life in this world. No matter what we are doing we are called to work to the best of our abilities to give glory to God. Our job is to make the invisible God visible. We can do this through what we do and by how we do it.

As we discussed in the previous chapter, work makes us something better, those around us better, the object of our work, our organization, better, our industry better, our community better; and it makes the world a better place, where we build up hearts of love and lives of shalom. Work gives us opportunity to fulfill parts of our design, a means to change us and develop us into our God-given potential, an opportunity to image God, the original Creator and ongoing Worker, an opportunity to become more like Jesus, the perfect embodiment of God's image, an opportunity to use our gifts in service for a greater good, ultimately glorifying God and bringing shalom to ourselves and the world around us.

CHAPTER 9

WHAT IS A GOOD PLACE?

A Good Place is a place where individual people flourish, organizations thrive, and communities prosper. Good Places are where individuals, organizations, and communities experience life the way God intends it in each of these three realms: people, organizations, and communities.

People experience a life of purpose, meaning, and fulfillment, filled with joy, life abundant and full (John 10:10; 15:11). At work, we honor and care for each other as equally valuable persons; building up hearts of love and lives of shalom; providing training, education, and development opportunities; experiencing joy in and through our work; providing quality of life for members of our organizations and their families.

In **organizations** we experience collective alignment of people, systems, resources, etc. toward the fulfillment of a shared purpose in a way that is more efficient, effective, healthy, and sustainable. In organizations, we experience meaningful and fulfilling work in a way that makes ourselves and those we work with something better, something that we cannot be on our own, allowing God to continue to create in us and through us. We experience opportunities to support our living in the world, provide for our physical sustenance, develop our full potential, build up who we are as individuals (our gifts, talents, etc.), care for others, and help make the world a better place. We can experience all of these through the work we do in organizations.

In **communities** we experience safety, well-being, and opportunities as well as encouragement of lifelong learning and development (physically, spiritually, relationally, emotionally, psychologically, educationally, vocationally, financially). This is where rights are protected and mutual respect is observed; where we serve, support, and provide for others; where we overcome evil with good, family is valued, and housing and community areas are safe, healthy, beautiful, and sustainable.

In short, we experience hearts of love and lives of shalom in each of the above three realms. We experience harmony (and/or harmonious relationships) with God, with each other and with creation; a deep sense of peace, completeness, wholeness, richness, wellbeing, and beauty.

CHAPTER 10

THE PURPOSE OF GOOD PLACE ORGANIZATIONS

The purpose of all Good Place organizations is to lead, operate, and build up organizations, deriving, aligning, and applying Biblical principles and values in organizational life that achieves (at least) the following three foundational aims:

1. **Valuing people** in general by honoring, respecting, loving, and caring for each other and others, as all people are made in the image of God (Genesis 1:27) and possess inherent value as persons. Valuing people specifically in a way that trains them to be fully competent and optimally perform in their job role, educates them beyond job training so they understand why their role is important and valuably contributes and aligns with the overall purpose of the organization, and provides opportunity and encouragement for people to develop to their full potential, fulfilling what they can become. Building a place where people love to work and engage in building a culture and community of organizational life together.

2. **Building up Good Places in the communities** where we work and live, making the world a better place and building up hearts of love and lives of shalom through the work the organization does, the business we are in, the products and services we provide, the skills the organization develops, and the methods and tools the organization uses to build Good Places. These could mean communities where we live and work geographically or where we interact relationally around a common interest. The desire is that others look at Good Place organizations and desire the same aims and adopt the same methods to achieve those aims, multiplying the effect of making the world a better place.

3. **Being economically regenerative,** which means that the organization is financially viable and sustainable and the surplus funds and resources it produces are used to reinvest in itself and its members to enhance health, growth, innovation, improvement, etc. It also may be invested in building up other Good Place organizations. The desire and motivation to create surplus funds and resources is to employ more people and build more Good Places, giving more people an opportunity to experience Good Place, versus hiring more people simply to increase profits. In short, we need to be economically regenerative in order to fund the other two aims.

In summary, through valuing people and building up Good Places through the means of the organizational business we choose to be in, these in turn produce the funds and resources to be economically regenerative. Said another way, the reason we create surplus is to value people and build up Good Places.

CHAPTER 11

THE 10 AREAS OF STEWARDING
A GOOD PLACE ORGANIZATION

The purpose of this chapter is to provide methods and tools to bring about the purpose, principles, and values derived from God's Word, apply them to organizational life and achieve, at least, the three aims of all Good Place organizations. These methods and tools are designed to coherently align and work together to achieve those aims, briefly summarized as follows:

1. Value people

2. Build up Good Places

3. Be economically regenerative

Many of the methods and tools in *The 10 Areas of Stewarding a Good Place Organization* are not entirely new or completely unique. If you have read any business book or taken a business class, you will most likely recognize some of the concepts we describe in *The 10 Areas*. However, there are two central and critical points of distinction that cannot be overlooked and that we believe are absolutely essential in our thinking, leading, and operating of Good Place organizations.

The first, as you can probably already imagine, is purpose and aim . The methods and tools of *The 10 Areas* are uniquely designed to work together toward fulfilling the specific purpose and bring about the specific three aims already mentioned. We believe that purpose and those aims are Biblically derived. *The 10 Areas* provide methods and tools and direct efforts toward achieving a Biblical definition of organizational success—what success looks like in God's economy. The aims described above are different from the purpose and aims of most for-profit organizations in the world today, where success is based on building owner or shareholder wealth or return on shareholder investment, solely defined in financial terms.

The second point of distinction is that there is intended connection, coordination, coherence, and comprehensiveness in the design and assembly of *The 10 Areas*, especially why and how they integrate with one another, work together, and have common themes and applications throughout to offer an overall and holistic approach to building up Good Place organizations and organizational life.

The 10 Areas of Stewarding a Good Place Organization are as follows:

1. Charter
2. Leadership
3. Managing Systems
4. Training, Education, and Development
5. Stewardship Planning
6. Financial Management
7. Managing Innovation
8. Managing Internal and External Communication
9. Managing the Business Formula
10. Community Engagement

We believe that the methods and tools in *The 10 Areas* are *a way* to achieve these aims, not *the only way*. There may be (and most likely are) other ways to achieve these aims. However, as shared previously, *The 10 Areas* are methods and tools that have been specifically designed and assembled to coherently work together to fulfill these specific purposes and achieve these specific aims. There are many other ways you can choose, especially those we have learned from the latest *New York Times* best-selling business book, our educational institutions, and/or from the proverbial "industry best practices" of corporate America. Unfortunately, corporate America has entirely different purposes and different aims than a Good Place.

So, this prompts a question: If our desire is to build a Good Place organization (or at least one that has similar purposes and aims), why would we uncritically choose methods and tools that were designed to accomplish completely different purposes and aims?

Within *The 10 Areas of Stewarding a Good Place Organization*, the first three areas make up the foundational concepts needed to understand, apply, train, and integrate throughout the organization when building a Good Place organization. These concepts include *Charter* at the organizational level and the associated Key Outcomes and Results, *Leadership* at the management level, and *Managing Systems* throughout the organization. The successive seven areas are specific applications of *Managing Systems*. As mentioned earlier, all ten areas have been intentionally assembled, connected, and coordinated in such a way as to bring about the overall aims of a Good Place organization and any additional unique aims of the organization based on the business it is in (figure 1).

Figure 1. The 10 Areas of Stewarding a Good Place Organization

CHAPTER 11

AREA 1: CHARTER

GOD IS ALWAYS PURPOSEFUL.

The Lord has made everything for its purpose...
Proverbs 16:4a

Biblical Summary

Whether the verses in the Bible on this topic apply to creation in general, to all people for all time, or to a specific people for a specific time, we can see that God is purposeful and has purpose for His creation and for the people placed in creation to live and work. The Westminster Shorter Catechism summarizes the whole of the Bible regarding the purpose of people in the following question and answer:

> Q: What is the chief end of man?
>
> A: The chief end of man is to glorify God and to enjoy Him forever.[13]

Another way to state the purpose of life is to seek and allow God's continuing creation (grace) in ourselves and through our lives in the world. God created us for this and doing so glorifies Him. (For further investigation regarding verses that represent the narrative or storyline of the Bible regarding this topic, see Appendix 2.)

Principles and Values

There is a pervasive theme in the Bible on this topic, describing a God who is Creator, Designer, Architect, and Owner of all things and who has purpose for His creation and aims we should be endeavoring toward. The Bible shares that these purposes and aims will never be stopped. The Bible also gives value guidance (or commands) as to how to view and carry out the means we choose to fulfill these purposes and aims.

The Bible shares what some of those purposes and aims should be, such as caring for God's creation and glorifying Him in everything we do, doing good works, doing justice, loving kindness, being humble, being of like mind with one another, and doing all in love. As leaders of a Good Place organization, we are to steward well that which God has entrusted to us, do good work, develop ourselves and those around us, and do these things to glorify and exalt Him. This includes and should be the intent of the Charter of the organization.

---

13   Westminster Assembly, D. F. Kelly, P. B. Rollinson, and F. T. Marsh, *The Westminster Shorter Catechism in Modern English* (Phillipsburg, N.J: Presbyterian and Reformed Publishing, 1986).

As we will learn later when applying the principles and determining the significant components of a Charter, we could easily describe the Good News of Bible in a similar fashion. In the Bible (and as described in chapter 6, "A Brief Storyline of the Good News of the Bible"), we see a metanarrative of God's purpose unfolding where God provides unmerited benefit to us, His creation, through His immense grace and because of His great love by solving the problem of sin and its eternal consequences at the cost of His own Son.

Therefore, we believe it is important to start with the "words at the top." In a Good Place, we call those words a *Charter*. A Charter is the embodiment of the characteristics of the purpose, vision, mission, aim, values, inspiration, and anything else that expresses what the organization desires to be and do. It is a statement that provides the "aim" of the entire organization as a system (not a hierarchy). It provides the direction we use to "chart" the course of the organization.

The Charter communicates and should answer such questions as:

- Why does this organization exist?
- To what "ends" does this organization exist?
- What difference will the organization make?
- What is this organization to achieve?
- What unique benefits are we providing and for whom?
- How will the world be different because the organization exists?
- In what areas should we direct our efforts toward the organization's growth?
- What are the values of the organization that guide behavior and culture?
- Who should be interested in joining this organization?

A Charter answers the main question: "Why does this organization exist?" It also addresses the several "critical questions" consultant and author, Patrick Lencioni believes all organizations should answer to create clarity and as a major component of a healthy organization: (1) Why do we exist? (2) How do we behave? (3) What do we do? (4) How will we succeed? (and/or how will we know we are succeeding?) (5) What is most important, right now? and (6) Who must do what?[14] As we will further experience in the "Practical Application for Leaders" segment of this section, the Charter addresses questions 1 (purpose and aim), 2 (behavioral values and/or guiding principles), 3 (vision and mission), and lends itself to accurately addressing 4 (Key Outcomes and Results). Question 5 can be answered in the *Stewardship Planning* section and question 6 in the *Managing Systems* section.

---

14   Patrick Lencioni, *The Advantage: Why Organizational Health Trumps Everything Else in Business* (Hoboken, NJ: Jossey-Bass, 2012).

In his book *Start with Why: How Great Leaders Inspire Everyone to Take Action,* author and speaker Simon Sinek espouses a similar concept as reflected in the title of his book.[15] Before we take action or make a decision, we need to start by reminding ourselves of our *Charter,* our purpose, why we exist.

A Charter has many other attributes as it accomplishes the above characteristics. A Charter gives direction. It sets the tone. It shapes culture. It brings unity. It settles disputes. It creates clarity. It provides inspiration and alignment. It provides context to equip and empower, and accountability for those who work in the organization. Everything that anyone in the organization does should be aimed at fulfilling the Charter. Any activity in the organization not called for by the Charter (or that does not support it) could indicate poor leadership.

As you can see, the purposes of a Charter are many and weighty. Everything about the organization hangs on the Charter. For these reasons, there is no optimal size of a Charter. It can be as short or as long as it needs be to address its necessary elements and communicate them clearly, unambiguously, and compellingly to its internal audience.

In a Good Place organization, we start with Charter. The Charter is the purpose, aim, vision, mission, and values that guide and direct all we do. In a Good Place organization, we have three aims in our Charter. In short, they are as follows:

1. Value people in a way that provides opportunity and encouragement for people to develop to their full potential.

2. Build up Good Places in our communities.

3. Be economically regenerative.

Practical Application for Leaders

The purpose of a Charter is to communicate to internal stakeholders who the organization is, why the organization exists, what to expect from the organization, who should be interested in joining the organization, in what areas the organization directs its efforts and resources, and what is important and what is not. The Charter is the embodiment of the characteristics of the purpose, vision, mission, aim, values, inspiration, and anything else that expresses what the organization desires to be and do. The Charter gives direction, sets the tone, shapes culture, settles disputes, brings clarity, provides inspiration and alignment, and provides context to equip, empower, and establish accountability for those who work in the organization.

A further word on the audience of the Charter. Given the purposes of a Charter, the audience is internal, specifically the members of the organization. The Charter is not a marketing message, an advertisement, an "elevator pitch," or the like.

---

15   Simon Sinek, *Start with Why: How Great Leaders Inspire Everyone to Take Action* (New York: Portfolio, 2009).

Certainly, you should use the Charter as the source of information and direction in these types of communications (see the section on *Managing Internal and External Communication*), but the Charter need not be word-smithed to meet the expectations or language of an external audience. In these communications it acts as the "source of truth" that all related internal and external communications should align with and be in support of.

First Steps in Charter

The first step in applying the concept of Charter to an organization is to determine what the Charter is. This can include creating one where one does not exist, refining one that is deficient or outdated, or confirming one that hits on all the areas we have discussed.

In determining what the Charter is, or should be, it is always wise to begin with prayer, asking God to lead and guide in this process of determining what His purpose for the organization is and using us and the organization to accomplish His ends.

It is also wise to understand some terms the Charter embodies so that we can determine an accurate and effective Charter. First and primary is *Purpose* and *Aim*. We define purpose as: the reason for which something exists or is done, made, or used; an intended or desired end or aim. Organizationally, the purpose directly answers the question: Why do we exist? It indirectly answers other questions: Who is this organization? What should we expect from this organization? Who should be interested in joining? In what areas should we direct our efforts? What do we value? What is important (and what is not)?

The second is *Vision* and *Mission*. Many organizations use these terms synonymously, while others separate them and have distinct definitions for each to serve their organizational needs. For our purposes, the common characteristics of these terms have to do with the idea of providing a concept of what the organization is to become, what it aspires to be, and thus they provide direction, guidance, and the like.

The third is *Guiding Principles* or *Behavioral Values*. These are the non-negotiables of behavior of the organization no matter the business it is in. Guiding principles or behavioral values can also be listed separately from the Charter to draw distinct attention and focus to them. These are the values of how people agree to interact with one another, the approach they agree to take in their work and while working in the organization. In a Good Place, these guiding principles/behavioral values are derived from the Bible, which has much to say about how we live in this world, how we view and interact with one another, how we view and interact with the world around us, how we view and interact in our work, how we perceive ourselves in all of these interactions, etc. Some organizations prefer to list these values separately from the purpose and vision portion of the Charter. That is completely fine. The idea is that the organization has these values, clearly communicates them so that people understand, and monitors their application and engagement as a key component to building Good Place culture.

Last is *Inspiration*. This characteristic should be inherent in any Charter or purpose statement. It should be compelling enough to call people and the organization of people to action, leading to accomplishing something that is worthy of our collective efforts and bigger than any one person. We all want to be a part of something bigger than ourselves, and the Charter is the statement that provides in words just that.

Determining the Charter

Start with prayer, asking God to use this process to help us determine the Charter He has for this organization.

Next, we walk through a series of questions like the ones listed above to help get the ideas out into the air. We then refine those ideas into a Charter addressing all of the necessary elements of a Charter, ensuring clear and compelling communication with our internal audience.

We often use the following "fill in the blank" statement to help us both construct a Charter and test to determine if we are addressing the baseline elements of the Charter:

The purpose of *THE ORGANIZATION* is to provide *THESE BENEFICIARIES* with *THESE BENEFITS* within *THESE GUIDING PRINCIPLES/BEHAVIORAL VALUES* commensurate with *THIS INVESTMENT/COST.*

Certainly, the Charter can be worded differently, but the statement above does the job of addressing the fundamentals efficiently and effectively, addressing the concepts of purpose, aim, vision, mission, and values.

The *Beneficiaries* of the organization can be anyone or anything that benefits from or receives the benefits of interacting with, engaging with, experiencing, or being a part of the organization, including but not limited to its products, services, offerings, and culture. Beneficiaries can be both external and internal to the organization. This certainly and most commonly includes those external to the organization (depending what kind of organization it is) like customers, the marketplace, students, etc. It could also include other things external to the organization such as vendors, suppliers, the community, our planet, and creation. Beneficiaries can also include those internal to the organization (depending on what kind of organization it is) who work in the organization such as employees, members, volunteers, contractors, etc. When constructing or testing a Charter, we can start with identifying the beneficiaries.

The *Benefits* are not features, or product, or service offerings, but the value provided by those things to the beneficiaries. What is the value the beneficiaries are receiving through the experience of interacting with, engaging with, or being a part of this organization? When constructing or testing a Charter, we can list the benefits each beneficiary should receive.

The *Guiding Principles* or *Behavioral Values* are the non-negotiables of how one will behave in the organization no matter what products or services are provided by the organization, what markets and customers it serves, etc. As stated previously, these are the values of how people agree to interact with one another, the approach they agree to take in their work and while working in the organization. In a Good Place, these guiding principles/

behavioral values are derived from the Bible, which has much to say about how we live in this world, how we view and interact with one another, how we view and interact with the world around us, how we view and interact in our work, and how we perceive ourselves in all of these interactions.

The *Investment* or *Cost* component of this statement simply reflects the financial or overall resource cost that is acceptable to provide the benefits to the beneficiaries. In a Good Place organization, it is essential to be a good steward of these resources to generate a commensurate return and to support and/or deliver economic regeneration, viability, sustainability, and/or a surplus to reinvest.

We can then put all of these components together to develop a thorough and cohesive Charter, or Charter statement, such as the examples below:

Examples of Charters

Example #1

The purpose of **The Good Housing Organization** is to provide safe, affordable, and value-giving housing to those who live in the City Community in a way that is honest, caring, and quality within at least a break-even annual budget.

Example #2

The purpose of **The Organic Food Company** is to:

- Provide health-promoting and nutrient-dense food to the community;
- Steward our resources by using regenerative food production practices; and
- Provide meaningful and fulfilling work that allows people to earn a living wage
- In a way that is economically regenerative.

Example #3

The purpose of **The City Movement** is to be a hub connecting, convening, communicating, and collaborating to unify the colors, cultures, and congregations, to see the people and communities of The City thrive and flourish, and do so in a way that is economically viable and sustainable.

Example #4

Good Place Holdings will grow thriving and sustainable organizations and encourage other organizations to apply Good Place principles and values which aim at:

- Valuing people over financial profits,
- The members of our organization are cared for and flourish both in and outside our organization,
- Fostering covenantal relationships with our customers and suppliers,
- The work we do to earn our living builds up Good Places in the communities where we work, and
- Ourselves and others can experience the continuing of creation in us and through our activities.

Figure 2 illustrates the concept of Charter, which acts as the ends the organization is endeavoring to fulfill and the embodiment of what is commonly referred to as "purpose, vision, mission, and values." It also illustrates how we can separate the values in the form of guiding principles and/or behavioral values, which act as non-negotiable "guard rails" of behavior and culture no matter what the organization is or the business you are in. This illustration also introduces some future concepts we will discuss later in the book such as means and the relationship between ends and means, especially in Governance and Management Leadership, and/or the means leadership chooses and manages to fulfill the purpose within the guiding principles and/or behavioral values in Managing Systems. Then, how leadership monitors the performance and production of the means (monitoring the Key Outcomes and Results), learns why the system is performing the way it is and producing what it is, implements appropriate improvements, and utilizes and builds on these concepts in how the organization does planning. These concepts will be applied and repeated, perhaps with slightly different words, in subsequent areas in *The 10 Areas, specifically Governance Leadership and Managing Systems.*

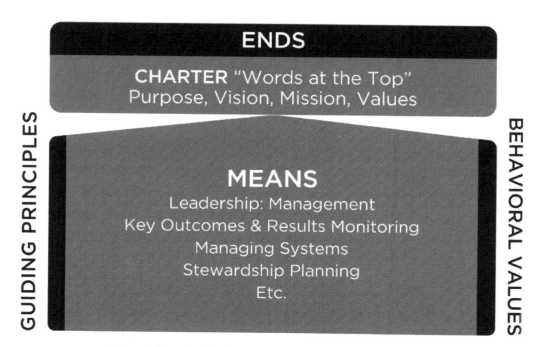

Figure 2. Organization Ends, Means, and Guiding Principles/Values

Monitor, Learn, and Improve to Fulfill the Charter: Key Outcomes and Results Dashboard

(NOTE: This section of Key Outcomes and Results will also apply in the area of Managing Systems, since an organization is an overall system, or more appropriately, an organized system of systems.)

Once the Charter is determined, how do we know if the organization is fulfilling it? How do you know if we are accomplishing the purpose for which the organization exists? To answer these questions, we need not look any further than the Charter itself for the clues and the operative words we should be focusing on to indicate if we are indeed fulfilling the Charter.

We identify these operative words from the Charter as Key Outcomes. How we measure or observe Key Outcomes, we call *Results*. Results can be measured or observed quantitatively or qualitatively and can be financial or non-financial. In short, Results are what the organization is producing and indicate successful achievement in the Key Outcomes categories as defined by the Charter. Said another way, this is a way to define success and monitor key success criteria. Key Outcomes and Results go by many names including: key performance indicators, success criteria, organizational key results, objectives, and key results.

A word of warning: Do not confuse Key Outcomes and Results with activities. Key Outcomes and Results are ends achieved or outputs produced. They are not means performed, activities finished, tasks done, or projects completed. This is probably the most significant distinction and, in our experience, the most challenging. For some reason, we want outcomes to be the completion of a task or project. Completing tasks and projects on time and on budget is very important, but unfortunately, we can complete tasks and not produce the expected results that the task was supposed to accomplish.

We then use the Key Outcomes and Results and build a dashboard report to monitor their achievement and the performance of the organization as it relates to the fulfillment of the Charter, the purpose of the organization.

To monitor the organization's performance and tell the story of how the organization is performing in fulfilling its Charter, we include specific data and informational elements in a Key Outcomes and Results Dashboard or report (figure 3).

KEY OUTCOMES & RESULTS DASHBOARD

KEY OUTCOMES & RESULTS	TIME	HISTORICAL RESULTS	PLANNED RESULTS	CURRENT RESULTS	STATUS	LEARN	IMPROVE
Outcome #1							
1.							
2.							
Outcome #2							
1.							
2.							
3.							
Outcome #3							
1.							
2.							
Outcome #4							
1.							
2.							

Figure 3. Organizational Key Outcomes and Results Dashboard

Definitions of Key Terms

Charter: "The Words at the Top," the purpose, vision, mission, aim, values, inspiration for our organization. This is similar to the purpose, which we will address under "Managing Systems."

Key Outcomes: Operative words from the Charter; key categories in which we should measure or observe results to determine Charter fulfillment.

Results: Reasonable (and brief) descriptions of the measurable or observable, quantitative or qualitative data indicators that indicate the achievement of an outcome. There may be multiple Results to indicate achievement in one Outcome. These may be financial or non-financial. Results are ideally described in terms of, or include, a unit of measure.

The following information should be provided for each Result:

Time: The timeframe to achieve and/or update Results—monthly, quarterly, annually, year-to-date, due date, etc. We can use multiple timeframes to track our Results in order to effectively tell the story of performance and achievement.

Historical Results: The Results data the system has historically produced in the defined timeframe(s). Results data is ideally recorded as a quantity and its associated unit of measure.

Planned Results: The discerned predicted Results data expected to be achieved in the defined timeframe(s) as determined through the impact of System Improvement(s), either stand-alone or thorough *Stewardship Planning*. Results data is ideally recorded as a quantity and its associated unit of measure.

Current Results: The Results data the system is actually and currently producing in the defined timeframe(s). Results data is ideally recorded as a quantity and its associated unit of measure.

Status: Comparison of the Current Results the system is producing with Planned and/or Historical Results, which gives an at-a-glance indicator as to whether our performance and achievement of the Result is ON TRACK, CAUTIONARY (we need to keep a close eye on this), or OFF TRACK. We can use simple "stoplight" indicators—green, yellow, or red—or whatever other symbols we would like to use to indicate this.

The following information should also be provided for each Result, or at least each Result that is significantly ON or OFF TRACK, or any other issue that needs to be highlighted:

Learn: The root cause(s) of why the system is producing the particular Results data. (We will talk more about "Learn" later in this section.)

Improve: System Improvements—the enhancements or corrections recommended and/or implemented based on the Current Results data produced, Status, and root cause. (We will talk more about "Improve" later in this section.)

We use these informational elements of the Key Outcomes and Results Dashboard to tell a story. For each Result, we tell the following story:

- What timeframe(s) should we measure or observe these Results?

- What has the organization/system produced in the past?

- What do we intelligently predict the organization/system will produce based on our planning (see Stewardship Planning) and the impact of Strategic Initiatives or System Improvements?

- What is the organization/system currently producing in that timeframe(s)?

- Is the Current Result on track, off track, cautionary (or some other status) compared to the Planned Results and/or the Historical Results?

- Why is the organization/system producing that Current Result?

- Should we do anything about it? Should we implement an improvement, an enhancement to a system producing on-track Results, or a corrective action to a system producing off-track Results?

There are three main audiences of the information in a Key Outcomes and Results Dashboard. One is the organizational leader—the person responsible and accountable for the fulfillment of the Charter and the means of operation. The second audience is the people who work in the organization, who use this information to understand how the organization is doing in fulfilling the Charter and achieving Key Outcomes and Results, and their valuable contribution to both. Third is the person or persons to whom the leader of the organization reports. This could be a board or another leader, in the case of a holdings company, etc.

Let's look at the Organic Food Company Charter provided above and work through an example of identifying Key Outcomes and Results:

The purpose of **The Organic Food Company** is to:

- Provide health-promoting and nutrient-dense food to the community;

- Steward our resources by using regenerative food production practices; and

- Provide meaningful and fulfilling work that allows people to earn a living wage

- In a way that is economically regenerative.

The Key Outcomes we would extrapolate from this Charter look like the following:

1. Health-promoting and nutrient-dense food to the community
2. Steward our resources by using regenerative food production practices
3. Meaningful and fulfilling work
4. Economically regenerative organization

The next step is to determine reasonable interpretations of how we will measure and/or observe the Results in each of the Key Outcome categories. For instance, we may determine the best ways to measure the Outcomes of "Health-promoting and nutrient-dense food to the community" are by measuring and/or observing the following Results (ideally described by a unit of measure):

*   Health-promoting food options
*   Key nutrient content
*   Nutrient density values
*   Customer (community members) health index
*   Number of new customers (the community)
*   Number of existing customers
*   Number of returning customers

To Manage, Learn, and Improve, we need to understand the system that produces the Key Outcomes and Results. In this case, the system is the organization (a system of systems). This involves developing the organizational system diagram and identifying and/or determining each of the informational components of the system to a level of detail that allows the leader to intimately understand and effectively manage how things work together to fulfill the purpose of the system and value the people working in the system, so as to not cause harm to the system or the people working in it.

Then, following the information asked for in the Key Outcomes and Results Dashboard, we "tell the story" of each Result, determining the timeframe(s) to monitor and update the Results, populating the Historical Results from the past and the Planned Results for the future (more on this in the section on *Stewardship Planning*), and updating the Current Results in those same timeframes. Then we Manage, Monitor, Learn, and Improve (see figure 4).

(NOTE: We will talk more about the organizational system diagram and walk through another example regarding identifying Key Outcomes and Results and populating the Dashboard in the section on *Managing Systems*.)

More about "Learn"

When monitoring Key Outcomes and Results, the most important facet is not just monitoring and comparing results but learning whether the system is producing stable and consistent or unstable and inconsistent Results, and understanding why in order to determine wise improvements. Our focus in learning is to clearly comprehend why the system is producing what it is producing, especially if it is producing a result outside expectations.

A System Manager should intimately understand the overall system and the components of the system to then understand why the system is producing what it is producing. This is called *root cause analysis* and is especially important when we find a Key Outcome and Result significantly outside expected averages and variation. In this case, we need to dive into the source or root cause. First, we determine where the cause is coming from, whether inside the system (a process step, activity, resource or tool, position, knowledge, skill, or ability, etc.) or from outside the system, an external influencer (such as markets, customers, suppliers, competitors, economy, government, regulations, world events, etc.). Once we determine whether the cause is internal or external, we then need to determine the nature of the cause, whether it is common or special.

If the cause is common, it means that the cause is inherent in or to the system and consistently affects every occurrence of the outcome result(s). If the cause is special, it means that the cause does not exist in the system all of the time, or it does not affect every occurrence but arises out of a special circumstance, usually external to the system.

It is wise to clearly understand if what the system is producing is outside expected averages and/or variation is coming from an internal or external cause(s), is a common cause or special cause, and if we have identified the true cause or just a symptom. It is sometimes as easy as asking the *why* question at least five times in order to get to the root. There are many other root cause analysis tools that can be administered to help determine the true cause.

More about "Improve"

If we learn the system is unstable, inconsistent, and/or unpredictable (i.e., produces unstable, inconsistent, or unpredictable results), the first and foremost improvement is to stabilize the system until we experience consistent and predictable results.

When the system is producing stable, consistent, and predictable results, our objective then is to simply make improvements that raise or lower the average based on the "game" we are playing. Are we bowling, where a higher average is desired? Or are we golfing, where a lower average is desired? We then look to narrow the range of variation and lower the standard deviation.

If we learn that the cause of performance is common, we would then improve the system through corrective action or enhancement. If we learn that the cause is special, we would then address the unique event appropriately, but not make a permanent change to the system.

However, if we initiate a change to the system, thinking we are making an improvement, without understanding the root cause—whether it is common or special, or treating a special cause as common—we are tampering with the system. We are simply reacting without thoughtfully responding. More than likely, this will actually cause more harm than good. And one of the first rules when managing a system is "first do no harm."

If, after we Learn, we determine to implement an improvement (an enhancement to a Key Outcome and Result that is "on track" or a corrective action to a Key Outcome and Result that is "off track"), we will need to determine what to change (as informed by root cause analysis), how to change (enhance or correct), and, sometimes most importantly, when to change. We then monitor the impact of that improvement for the associated Key Outcome and Result it was intended to improve to continuously Learn and Improve. Remember, it is only an improvement when it positively impacts the Key Outcomes and Results it was intended to improve.

Therefore, at this overall organizational Charter level, the Planning, Managing, Monitoring, Learning, and Improving process becomes circular and results in continuous stewardship, improvement, and ongoing (not one-time or annual) planning. Adjustments can occur throughout the year, which in turn gives greater probability of successful Plan and Outcomes and Results achievement and Charter fulfillment. (We will revisit this in the sections on *Managing Systems* and *Stewardship Planning*.) See figure 4 to further illustrate this concept.

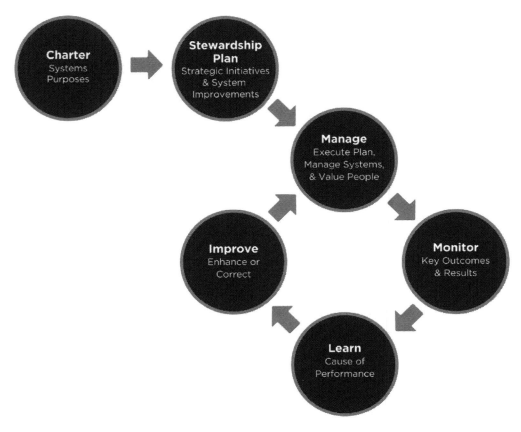

Figure 4. Stewardship Cycle: Plan, Manage, Monitor, Learn, and Improve

Analogy from Sport

At this time, we want to begin to put together some of the concepts we have learned and will learn as we read through this book in a way that will help with clarity and understanding. One of the best ways to do that is through story or analogy. We'll go with the analogy for this.

For those who have coached, played, or watched team sports, we all can easily identify the simple and fairly straightforward purpose and vision of most team sports, which is to win within the rules of the game. If you are a little deeper in your thinking about sport, the purpose might be something more about competing with excellence (of which winning might be a Key Outcome) while building character and developing the athletes. For the purpose of our analogy, let's keep it simple and say that winning is one of the purposes we desire to fulfill and a Key Outcome we desire to achieve when playing sports (while agreeing that in a bigger picture "winning" or "success" in sports can be defined in many ways). In sports, we also know that the scoreboard (or the score book) possesses the information we need to know in order to determine whether this purpose is being fulfilled, and Key Outcomes are being achieved by the team on a game-by-game basis. We can see who is winning or who is losing based on the data measurements presented on the scoreboard in terms of key results like number of points, goals, etc. We also know whether we are playing within the rules, or with character per se, based on the results presented on the scoreboard in terms of number or type of penalties or fouls.

If we are keeping track of this over time, we know historically what our results have been (what is our historical record for the season or last season). We also know that most likely the coach of the team has put together a game plan (the *system*, if you will, which we will discuss in a later section of *The 10 Areas*) to fulfill the purpose of the team and achieve Key Outcomes and Results, namely, to win games within the rules. The coach may have even put in some improvements in our game plan based on our performance last season, or the last game, or the last half, etc. (More on that in the sections on *Managing Systems* and *Stewardship Planning*.) The coach would then engage in practices to equip the team to carry out the game plan (the *training*, if you will, which we will also discuss in a later section).

Based on the game plan, we predict we are going to win (or win so many games, hopefully better than last season). Then our team must go and execute the game plan in a way that gives us the best probability to fulfill our purpose and achieve the Key Outcomes and Results.

What we are focused on at this point in our analogy are the Key Outcomes and Results we are desiring to achieve based on the Charter, or purpose, of our team, which are presented on the scoreboard indicating whether we are winning or losing the game (whether we are "on track" or "off track" regarding the achievement of planned performance). This is basically how we monitor the Key Outcomes and Results to "keep score" of the game we are playing to determine if we are fulfilling the purpose of our team.

We know this is a simplistic analogy and will break down as you go into further depth on this subject, but hopefully this gives a simpler context for us to get the idea and concepts as we move through them.

CHAPTER 11

AREA 2: LEADERSHIP

LEADERSHIP IS A ROLE TO SERVE.

When he had washed their feet and put on his outer garments and resumed his place, he said to them, "Do you understand what I have done to you? You call me Teacher and Lord, and you are right, for so I am. If I then, your Lord and Teacher, have washed your feet, you also ought to wash one another's feet. For I have given you an example, that you also should do just as I have done to you.

John 13:12–15

Biblical Summary

Throughout the Bible, we witness many leaders demonstrating Biblical leadership character and traits. The first and foremast person in the Bible to whom we should look for leadership traits is Jesus. We can then look at others, including Paul, who clearly stated that we should follow him as he followed Jesus (1 Corinthians 11:1). We can also look at many others like Peter, John, Moses, Esther, Nehemiah, Ruth, and Solomon to compile a fairly comprehensive list of Biblical leadership characteristics we can use to lead Good Place organizations.

In Jesus's most famous speech, known as the Sermon on the Mount, He clearly lays out character traits He values, and we should espouse them in our lives and, therefore, in our leadership . (For further investigation regarding verses that represent the narrative or storyline of the Bible regarding this topic, see Appendix 2.)

Principles and Values

We see in the life of Jesus, and particularly illustrated by the Sermon on the Mount, that He invested in people, and specifically a diverse group of people. Some would even describe this group of people as unqualified for the job Jesus was equipping them to do. Jesus built authentic relationships with them. He shared a vision of something much larger than themselves. He trained, educated, and equipped them for the mission and tasks set before them. He developed them into something far greater than they ever imagined, utilizing their gifts and fulfilling their God-given potential. He then released them to carry out the mission with authority and responsibility. He modeled all that He was teaching and developing in them. He held them accountable. He loved people. He was never diverted from His mission all the way to the end when His mission on earth was finally accomplished. Lastly, Jesus had a plan that He shared with His followers for the mission to continue when He was not with them any longer, and they carried it out long after He was gone. We have the privilege and honor of being recipients of this plan and co-laborers in the mission still being carried out today.

Leadership in a Good Place organization follows these principles. Leadership is not about external reward, popularity, or influence for selfish gain. Leadership is about stewardship and sacrifice. Leadership is about serving, serving people and a greater purpose.

From the Sermon on the Mount and the verses above, and many more like them, we can see that the characteristics of a leader (i.e., Biblical leadership) are not about technique, methodologies, or style. We see that leadership is a role for serving others, which requires character. Here is a non-exhaustive list of leadership character traits Good Place leaders should be passionately pursuing, if not already possess:

- Serving with a servant's heart
- Humility
- Love
- Gentle
- Joyful
- Peaceful
- Patient
- Self-controlled
- Relationally healthy
- Does what is right and above reproach
- Demonstrates integrity
- Competent
- Skillful
- Authoritative (not authoritarian)
- Seeks and demonstrates wisdom and discernment
- Kind
- Trustworthy
- Takes initiative
- Passionate
- Prayerful
- Strong and courageous
- Optimistic
- Enthusiastic and energetic
- Cultivates unity
- Empathetic
- Disciplined
- Emotionally intelligent—knows themselves and others
- Learner and teachable
- Accountable
- Submissive to authority
- Good steward
- Mature
- Purposeful
- Thankful

Beyond the character of a leader, we can derive further purposes, roles, and responsibilities of a leader. The purpose of leadership is to steward the organization, serve its people, and determine how the organization fulfills its purpose. Leaders influence and work in a way that motivates people to want to do the right things. Leaders seek to understand the people they lead and do what is in the best interest of the organization, but not just to facilitate the will of the group. An important aspect of leadership includes being in touch with and knowing those they lead in order to be familiar with their working conditions, personal lives, range of emotions, current attitudes, etc. We do this in large part because we are human, and we are designed to relate and for healthy relationships. Thus, leadership requires the skills to build healthy relationships. It requires us to know and be known by those with whom we work. This is where concepts such as trust, transparency, vulnerability, healthy conflict, accountability, clarity, and commitment to the shared purpose and common aim of the organization come into play as a leader builds up the members of the organization, valuing the people of the organization and stewarding the organization to fulfill its purpose.

Ultimately, leaders tend to the health of the organization by tending to the growth and development of the members, taking care of the people of the organization, and managing the systems within which they work.

In a Good Place organization, everything leaders do is directed at accomplishing the three aims of a Good Place organization, leading and operating by Biblical principles and values to (1) value people, (2) build up Good Places, and (3) be economically regenerative. *The 10 Areas* are simply methods and tools leaders use to accomplish these three aims.

Analogy from Sport

Coaching is just one form of leadership, but it has characteristics that can guide people in all other forms of leadership. Coaches inspire their athletes to achieve performance beyond what they (the athletes) previously thought themselves capable of. Coaches work through their team (the individual members coming together as one unit) to accomplish the purpose and aims of the team. Coaches model, inspire, care, relate, are known, equip, and empower.

Practical Application for Leaders

The overall purpose of leadership in a Good Place organization is to serve to ensure the Charter is fulfilled within some guiding principles while practicing certain behavioral values. In a Good Place organization, everything leaders do is ultimately directed at accomplishing the three aims of a Good Place organization (valuing people, building up Good Places, and being economically regenerative) through the unique business the organization is in, leading and operating by Biblical principles and values, ultimately making the world a better place.

We apply the principles and values described above, and the character of the leader, to two categories of formal leadership in a Good Place organization:

1. Governance—provided by a Policy Governance Board
2. Management—provided by the CEO/President and their organizational leaders

As a general introduction to these two categories, we say that Governance is exercised by the Board and Management is exercised the CEO (which can go by many titles such as President, Executive Director, etc.) and the Staff they steward and lead. We have found that organizations work best when the Board attends to Governance, the CEO and Staff attends to Management, and neither meddles in the other's role. The Management role is accountable to Governance and the Governance role is accountable to Ownership.

In a Policy Governance model, the Board represents the will and desires of the moral owner(s) of the organization and governs by defining, in written policy, the ends to be accomplished by the Organization and the means to be avoided while accomplishing those ends. An *end* is a benefit for a defined recipient at an acceptable cost. And for our context, a *means* is anything that is not an end. The Board does not get involved in the Management world of means beyond identifying what means may not be used, even if they were effective, in producing the specified ends. These are called Executive Limitations. The Management role, then, is to reasonably interpret the ends and determine the means to achieve them within these limitations. In short, Board Governance determines ends and Executive Limitations whereas Management determines means. See figure 5 to further illustrate this concept.

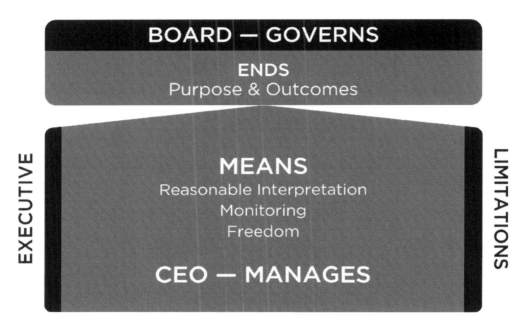

Figure 5. Board Governs Ends and Determines Executive Limitations;
CEO Manages Means within Executive Limitations

With some minor variations in wording and organizational level of application, you may have noticed this closely resembles and conceptually aligns with figure 2 in the previously discussed section on *Charter*. Again, these concepts will be applied and repeated, perhaps with slightly different words, in subsequent areas of *The 10 Areas*, specifically in the upcoming section on *Managing Systems*.

Governance Leadership at the Board level represents the moral owner of the organization, determines the ultimate ends of the organization, and ensures those ends are being achieved through means that do not violate certain values and principles. From a Biblical perspective, the ultimate moral owner is God, who is the Creator and owner of all things, and the role the Board plays represents the role and activity of God, who has a purpose for all created things and ensures that purpose gets accomplished in ways He defines as good.

Management Leadership at the CEO/President (and staff leadership) levels is delegated authority and responsibility from the Board to carry out the mission of the organization and accomplish the ends determined by the Board by, in turn, determining the means within and/or in alignment with the determined principles and values. Again, from a Biblical perspective, we can equate this management leadership role to the Biblical leaders mentioned earlier, who played this leadership role in their context, carrying out the will of the moral owner(s) and what they desire to achieve and, therefore, to us as leaders of a Good Place organization.

There is a bright line of authority and responsibility between these two leadership roles, between the board and management. In an ideal and pure form of policy governance, that line is not crossed, unless management invites the board into the means, perhaps as a volunteer or a specialist to help accomplish something. However, in so doing, the board member no longer acts in their board capacity, but is there at the good pleasure of management and reports accordingly.

A Deeper Dive into Governance Leadership

When we talk about governance leadership, we are specifically talking about Board Leadership. The form of Board Leadership we espouse at Good Place is a close derivation of the Carver Policy Governance model. The Carver model was introduced by John Carver in his book *Boards that Make a Difference.*[16] In his subsequent book, *Reinventing Your Board,*[17] the Carvers explain this model in more detail and give implementation guidance. Over the years, although we follow the Carver Policy Governance model fairly closely, we have made modifications to this approach to align and connect them with the principles, values, and aims of Good Place and *The 10 Areas of Stewarding a Good Place Organization*, namely *Managing Systems* (which we will talk about in the next section). Those who may be Carver model purists will find some separation in this regard. We believe that the assembly of concepts that formulate this form of Board Policy Governance Leadership is highly effective at stewarding organizations from the Board (governance leadership) in and through the CEO (management leadership) and closely represents principles and values of Biblical leadership.

The purpose of a Governance Board is to represent ownership; delineate Board and CEO roles including relationship, authority, and responsibilities; communicate clear and reasonable expectations of the Board and the CEO; establish alignment and accountability regarding fulfilling the purpose and achieving the Key Outcomes and Results of the organization; perpetuate and sustain the essence and culture of the organization beyond dependence on an individual or individuals; engender more effective and efficient use of time, talent, and resources; provide a framework and freedom to do the right things and focus on the main things; and integrate coherently with the other areas of *The 10 Areas of Stewarding* a *Good Place Organization* to achieve the aims of Good Place organizations. The Governance Board accomplishes this by establishing and governing through creating policies and selecting the CEO to carry out and fulfill the purpose of the organization.

The Board represents and is accountable to the ownership of the organization. Whether that ownership is actual and legal or those with moral ownership roles. In short, the Board's role is to represent the interests of Ownership—actual or moral.

---

16 John Carver, *Boards that Make a Difference, 3rd ed.* (Hoboken, NJ: Jossey-Bass, 2006).

17 John Carver and Mariam M. Carver, *Reinventing Your Board, rev. ed.* (Hoboken, NJ: Jossey-Bass, 2006).

It is imperative for the Board to identify whom the owners of the organization are and know them and their desire for the organization in order to represent them well. The Board is also to establish and live out the purpose of the organization.

To fulfill the purposes of Governance, and to accurately represent the ownership of the organization, the Board creates policies in four areas: Governance Process Policies, Board-Management Delegation Policies, Executive Limitations Policies, and an Ends Policy.[18] The first two areas are related to the Board and its function. The last two policy areas are provided by the Board, then assigned and delegated to the CEO/Management for their reasonable interpretation and determination of the means to achieve (figure 6).

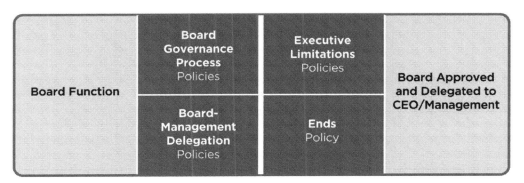

Figure 6. The Four Policy Categories of Policy Governance

Governance Process Policies: state the purpose and role of the Governance Board as it relates to representing ownership, ensuring ends are achieved and the purpose of the organization fulfilled while avoiding prohibited actions or behavior. They also state the process by which the Board will accomplish their role.

Board-Management Delegation Policies: describe assignment of policies from the Board to the CEO, the delegation to the CEO of the responsibility and commensurate authority to determine the means with which to accomplish the ends within the Executive Limitations, the monitoring of the performance of the CEO and the organization regarding the policies assigned and delegated, and the accountability of the CEO to and from the Board.

Executive Limitations Policies: are the prohibited means assigned to and committed to by the CEO. These can also be viewed as behavioral values, behavioral non-negotiables, or guiding principles of the organization. No matter what business you are in, these are the means that are prohibited for the CEO to engage in when determining the means to achieve the ends. These limitations are stated in the negative as it is usually easier and clearer to state the limited number of things one is not allowed to do versus all of the things one is allowed to do. The limitations are usually addressed in the following categories, which can be combined and can include but are not limited to: financial planning and condition, treatment of staff, treatment of customers, treatment of vendors and suppliers, asset protection, treatment of creation, community impact, compensation and benefits, communication and support to the Board, and succession.

18   John Carver and Mariam M. Carver, *Reinventing Your Board, rev. ed.* (Hoboken, NJ: Jossey-Bass, 2006).

Ends Policy: is the ultimate purpose for which the organization exists, by which all outcomes and results are derived (and for which they are monitored), and to which all activities are aimed. The Ends Policy, in its simplest form, describes that the organization exists to provide these benefits to these beneficiaries at a commensurate and/or acceptable cost of resources. (A point of note from our discussion is that a Charter for an organization is of the same kind as an Ends Policy.)

The Board writes these policies in levels, starting with the most basic and comprehensive policy, then going to whatever deeper level of detail it feels is necessary, such that it is willing to accept "any reasonable interpretation" of the written policy. At whatever level the Board is comfortable with any reasonable interpretation of a policy by the CEO, further detail is not necessary. The more specific and detailed the policies become, the less room and freedom the CEO has to work to accomplish the mission. The Board only prescribes ends to be accomplished and means to be avoided. The Board never prescribes means by which to accomplish ends, which is the responsibility of the CEO.

Once policies are developed and approved by the Board, the CEO describes their interpretation of the individual policies in an operational definition, giving support and/or rationale for that interpretation; and proposes by what measures it will be determined that they have met the Policy requirements. We commonly call these Key Outcomes and Results. (These concepts and words—Purpose, Key Outcomes and Results, etc.— should look familiar from our discussion on Charter and will be visited again and again as we discuss and apply *Managing Systems* later in the book.) The CEO then determines what means they will use to accomplish the ends. Practically speaking, this has to do with how the CEO will design and build the organization and organizational systems, staffing, strategy, planning, structure, etc. A point to note here is that many non-profit organizations utilize Board members as volunteer operational staff. When this occurs, the Board member is no longer a Board member while volunteering, but rather a volunteer who is asked to serve at the pleasure of the CEO. This keeps clear the bright line between the purpose and function of the Board and the CEO and eliminates any unnecessary confusion and/or meddling in each other's roles, responsibilities, and authority.

The Board then determines how it will monitor the Policy as interpreted, with measurements defined by and frequency determined by the CEO. The Board can use internally generated reports from Management, its own direct observation or measurement, or third-party survey, inspection, or audit. These monitoring reports also serve to evaluate the performance of the CEO, since these policies provide the clear, unambiguous expectations for which the CEO was hired and has been delegated the authority and responsibility to achieve.

In summary, the Governance Board does four things:

1. Writes policies describing what is to be accomplished, in particular the ends/ purpose within Executive Limitations to whatever level of detail necessary to fulfill the ends of the organization.

2. Assigns and Delegates policies to the CEO.

3. Approves the CEO's reasonable interpretations, usually in the form of Key Outcomes and Results (which could also include applicable rationale).

4. Evaluates monitoring reports—checking to make sure the ends/purpose is being fulfilled by Key Outcomes and Results being achieved.

In doing the above four things, the Governance Board is guided by the following ten principles:

1. The Board stands in for those who morally own the organization.

2. The Board speaks with one voice or not at all. The Board will allow no officer, committee, or individual on the Board to come between the Board and its CEO.

3. The Board directs the organization by addressing the Ends and Executive Limitation Policies to the CEO.

4. The Board instructs no staff but the CEO.

5. Ends* and means are distinguished from each other only according to whether an issue describes three key elements:

   1. what outcomes or difference is to be produced,

   2. for whom it is to be produced, and

   3. the value or cost of the outcome.

* A few quick notes regarding ends:

- An issue that describes one or more of these attributes is an ends issue.

- An issue that does not describe one or more of these attributes is a means issue.

- That a matter is important does not make it an ends issue. That the Board wishes to control an issue does not make it an ends issue. That a matter is controlled by law or custom does not make it an ends issue.

6. The Board controls ends issues positively—by prescribing certain ones.

7. The Board controls means (and staff) issues negatively—by prohibiting certain ones. These are known as Executive Limitations.

8. The Board defines policy issues from the most general level of specificity to that more detailed level where it can assign and delegate any reasonable interpretation of its words.

9. The Board may change the level of its policy making at any time.

10. The Board monitors performance against its policy words.

In our journey developing and/or serving on Policy Governance-type Boards, we have assembled the following topical steps that should be addressed when implementing a Policy Governance Board.

BOARD POLICY GOVERNANCE: Steps to Implementation

I. Policy Governance—Board Clarity and Commitment

II. Policy Governance—Overview Training

    A. Overview of Policy Governance—purpose and description

    B. Leadership—Governance and Management

    C. 10 Principles of Policy Governance

    D. Purpose and roles of the Board

    E. Purpose and role of the CEO

III. Policy Governance—4 Quadrant Policy Training

    A. Overview of Policy Categories and the degree of desired prescribed policy detail ("Nesting Bowls" concept)

    B. Quadrant 1: Board-Management delegation

    C. Quadrant 2: Governance process

    D. Quadrant 3: Executive Limitations

    E. Quadrant 4: Ends

IV. Board-Management Delegation Policies

    A. Topical training review

    B. Review examples and templates

    C. Board: write, review, and approve global policies

    D. Board: write, review, and approve level 2, 3, etc. policies

V. Governance Process Policies

    A. Topical training review

    B. Review examples and templates

    C. Board: write, review, and approve global policies

    D. Board: write, review, and approve level 2, 3, etc. policies

VI. Ends Policy

    A. Review examples and templates

    B. Board: write, review, and approve global Ends Policy statement and assign to CEO

    C. CEO: write "reasonable interpretation" of Ends Policy, either in the form of a report or Key Outcomes and Results Dashboard

    D. Board: review, feedback, revise, and approve CEO interpretation

VII. Executive Limitations Policies

    A. Topical training review

    B. Review examples and templates

    C. Board: write, review, and approve global Executive Limitations policies and assign to CEO

    D. Board: write, review, and approve level 2, 3, etc. policies

    E. CEO: writes "reasonable interpretations" of Executive Limitations policy statements

    F. Board: review, feedback, revise, and approve CEO interpretation

VIII. Board Write and/or Assemble Policy Governance Board Manual

IX. Ends Policy Board Monitoring Reports—set calendar

    A. Topical training review

    B. Review training, examples, and templates

    C. CEO writes Ends Policy Board Monitoring Report—global policy statement(s), CEO interpretation, rationale (if necessary), data (update), status (update), analysis and correction (if "off track")

    D. Board: receive, evaluate, discuss, and approve CEO Board Monitoring Report for the Ends Policy monthly, quarterly, and/or annually

X. Executive Limitations Policies Board Monitoring Reports—set calendar

    A. Topical training review

    B. CEO writes Executive Limitations Policies Board Monitoring Reports—global and level X policy statement(s), CEO interpretation for each statement, rationale (if necessary), for each statement, data (update) for each statement, status (update) for each statement, analysis and correction (if "off track") for each statement

    C. Board: receive, evaluate, discuss, and approve CEO Board Monitoring Report for 1 or 2 Executive Limitation Policies per meeting time on an annual rotation, except Financial Condition, which may be evaluated more frequently

XI. CEO Performance Assessment

    A. Culmination of CEO Board Monitoring Reports

    B. Annual

A Deeper Dive into Management Leadership

As discussed earlier, leadership is a role for serving people. Leaders also influence people and unite people and resources toward a shared purpose. In a Good Place organization, formal management leadership is responsible to steward well that which has been entrusted to them and the organization. Management leadership accomplishes this by determining how (the means) an organization fulfills its Charter and/or a system fulfills its purpose and serves people, both considered ends. In short, in a Good Place organization, management leaders have the authority and responsibility to manage systems (or the organization of systems) and value the people who work in the system, versus simply managing people or their individual tasks and activities. All leaders must manage; however, we have certainly experienced that not all managers are leaders.

In Managing Systems, management leaders are responsible to optimally organize processes, activities, people, tools, resources, skills, knowledge, etc., increasing the value of their labor, to achieve Key Outcomes and Results and, thus, fulfill the Charter of the organization and/or the purpose of the system. This means that management leaders have authority, responsibility, and accountability for the outcomes of the organization, or the outcomes of the system, more so than do individual employee members. Management leaders are also responsible for the continued management, health, and improvement of the organization and its systems. In doing so, management leaders first have the responsibility to do no harm. This means leaders, System Managers, understand the system they manage, the people they lead, and why each is performing the way that it is before making changes. We will talk more about this in the *Managing Systems* section of this book.

In valuing people, as previously discussed in the aims of all Good Place organizations, management leaders have the responsibility and authority to train, equip, align, empower, and encourage the people working in the organization (and/or system) to develop and reach their full potential. This means training to do their job the best they can; education beyond job training and to know why the job role is important and how it fits within the system(s) that is designed and organized to fulfill the Charter (purpose), thus being fully competent in their role; and finally, developing to fulfill their God-given potential and the person they can become. This means building a workplace community and organizational life that cares for people personally and professionally, developing an environment where people can flourish, and engaging in building up hearts of love and lives of shalom (for the benefit of the individual, organization, and community).

With Leadership being the second of *The 10 Areas*, we may have expected to have covered more ground in this section on *Management Leadership*. However, since the primary role and responsibilities of management leaders in a Good Place organization are to fulfill the Charter of the organization, manage the systems of the organization (whether a system of systems at the overall organizational level, or a single system at a department level), and value the members of the organization, each of the sections of chapter 11, especially *Managing Systems*, are all the responsibility of leadership. All leaders are responsible to build up Good Place organizations through *The 10 Areas of Stewarding a Good Place Organization*. Therefore, each of the sections of chapter 11 fall under the responsibility of management leaders.

CHAPTER 11

AREA 3: MANAGING SYSTEMS

CREATION IS DESIGNED TO WORK TOGETHER FOR A PURPOSE.

For just as the body is one and has many members, and all the members of the body, though many, are one body, so it is with Christ.

1 Corinthians 12:12

Biblical Summary

We see in God's Word—both in the storyline of the Bible and in God's creation—systemic design, the idea that many individual and integrated parts are organized in a way that they become one and work together to accomplish a larger, common purpose. The Bible also illustrates this concept when describing the Church as many parts yet one body. We see in the Bible that, first and foremast, God is Creator and Owner of all things. We, as human beings made in His image, are responsible and accountable to God to steward well that which He created and has given and entrusted to us to manage, tend, and oversee. We see that we are designed to work with and for a purpose and within a systematic context where we have a job yet do not just work for ourselves but work in connection with others for the betterment of each other and the world as co-creators and co-laborers with God. We were designed to work with excellence to grow and develop ourselves and others and bring glory to the Creator. (For further investigation regarding verses that represent the narrative or storyline of the Bible regarding this topic, see Appendix 2.)

Principles and Values

The concept of systems, systems thinking, and the components that make up systems is abundant throughout Scripture and in creation. We see and are thinking primarily of organic systems, not necessarily mechanistic systems. When we look at examples in the Bible and in nature, we see parts intended and designed to work together to fulfill some shared purpose, something bigger than the individual part on its own could accomplish. We see this in the body of Christ (the Church) and in the human body with its individual parts and collection of systems such as the respiratory system, circulatory system, nervous system, muscular system, skeletal system, etc. We see this in a garden and its plants where the system/process of photosynthesis keeps them alive and allows them to contribute to the life of others around them. The earth itself is made up of ecosystems that allow it to fulfill its purpose of sustaining life on our planet. In fact, the systems in nature and organic systems work so efficiently and effectively, people actually look to them to imitate their characteristics in order to optimize mechanistic systems and manufactured products. There is an entire field of study and application regarding this topic that is called *biomimicry*. We also see systems of leadership and the coordination of work to accomplish something greater than any one person could accomplish on their own. The examples of systems in Scripture and in our natural world are almost endless.

We have now learned about Charter, the purpose, vision, mission, values of an organization; and Leadership—those who serve, organize, manage, and have stewardship responsibility for the organization. Now we move to the methods and tools to define the means management leaders determine and manage to achieve Key Outcomes and Results, thus fulfilling the Charter of the organization they lead. Or, at other levels of the organization, the means management leaders determine and manage to achieve Key Outcomes and Results, thus fulfilling the purpose of the system they manage (usually a business unit or department, but also could be applied to a working group, cross-departmental function, team, etc.). W. Edwards Deming was famous for saying that "a system must have an aim. Without an aim there is no system."[19] The system is the means (the method) to achieve the ends (the aim or purpose), and the Key Outcomes and Results indicating fulfillment of the purpose.

This system thinking and approach provides a means to steward well that which we have been entrusted, to value people, to meaningfully align people to purpose, to experience sustainability beyond "hero leaders," to achieve stability and predictability and continuous improvement, and to engage, energize, equip, and empower people.

When talking about systems, then, we first say that every system has an aim, a purpose. We acknowledge that leadership and authority serve the aims of the system. And every organization is a system, not a hierarchy. You could also say, and perhaps this is more accurate, that an organization is an organized system of systems. Business units or departments are also systems, not hierarchies. A system is simply a network of interdependent components that work together to accomplish the purpose (or aim) of the system—the means chosen to achieve the desired outcomes. A system includes people working collaboratively and collectively to achieve a common aim. An organizational system is the work of a group toward fulfilling that shared purpose. Organizational systems produce Key Outcomes and Results that are measurable or observable, quantitative or qualitative key indicators or success criteria of the organization that indicate that the organization/system is fulfilling its Charter/purpose. We introduced the concept of Key Outcomes and Results and the methods and tools to monitor and track in the section on *Charter* and will apply it again in the practical application of *Managing Systems* below.

Organizational systems provide the means (the "how to") to organize people, skills, activities, resources, labor, etc. that work in the system in an efficient, effective, and optimal manner to produce the Key Outcomes and Results and, thus, fulfill its purpose, far more than individual or heroic effort. As we continue to Manage Systems (the means) and monitor the Key Outcomes and Results (the ends), throughout the year, we have a built-in mechanism to continuously improve the system and its outcomes. Our goal when it comes to Key Outcomes and Results is to improve the average and/or narrow the variation.

---

19   W. Edwards Deming, *The New Economics for Industry, Government, Education, 2nd ed.* (Cambridge, MA: MIT Press, 1994), 95–96.

As stated above, every system has a purpose. One of the foundational purposes of every system, or work process, is the good of the people it serves—the people served by the system's product and services (customers) or served by the system's needs for products and services (suppliers), and the people working in the system (members of the organization). Therefore, in a Good Place organization, we strive to manage systems and value people, versus just manage people. We call the latter (managing people) "heroics" as this form of leadership is usually based on a charismatic leader, an off-the-charts performer, or a micro-manager of activities and tasks and usually not replicable, sustainable, or consistent beyond the person related to achieving outcomes and results and fulfilling the purpose.

To manage systems and value people well, it requires knowledge of the individual components that make up the system, the interrelationships between component and other systems, and the people who work within the systems. As we have already stated, the first rule of Managing Systems is "first do no harm," which simply means, do not react and change things before you truly understand the system and what is causing the results the system is producing.

Practical Application for Leaders

A system is the work of a group working together toward a common purpose. Therefore, we refer to organizations as systems, not hierarchies. Every system has an aim, a purpose. For an organization to be effective, every member of the organization needs to understand the dynamics and the human physics of groups, utilizing their time, talent, and resources, working toward their common purpose. Those with formal authority in the organization need this understanding as well as the skills of identifying, equipping, and empowering people to achieve unity of aims, methods, and outcomes. Therefore, the purpose of Managing Systems in a Good Place organization is to steward well that which has been entrusted to the organization, providing the means to achieve the Key Outcomes and Results and thus fulfill the purpose of the system and the Charter of the organization and to value people.

As we walk through how we apply this Managing Systems thinking as a vital concept to building Good Place organizations, you will notice many concepts have some of their basis in the writings of W. Edwards Deming (1900–1993), who was an international consultant in quality and productivity management. If you would like more depth and background on systems and systems thinking, you may want to dive into a couple of Deming's books, *Out of Crisis and The New Economy for Industry, Government, Education.*

The first steps for an organization in Managing Systems is to identify the major systems that make up the organization and that are essential to produce the Key Outcomes and Results and thus fulfill the Charter. In a Good Place organization, these fall into two general categories of systems. First, the major organizational systems include general functions common to most organizations in some form or another. They include but are not limited to:

- Marketing
- Sales/Development
- Operations (Production and Delivery)

- Human Resources
- Finance
- Information Technology
- Legal

Second, we apply Managing Systems to the specifically applied systems of *The 10 Areas of Stewarding a Good Place Organization* which mainly include:

- Training, Education, and Development
- Stewardship Planning
- Financial Management
- Managing Innovation
- Managing Internal and External Communication
- Managing the Business Formula
- Community Engagement

These major systems can be identified and illustrated by a system overview diagram such as the example below (figure 7).

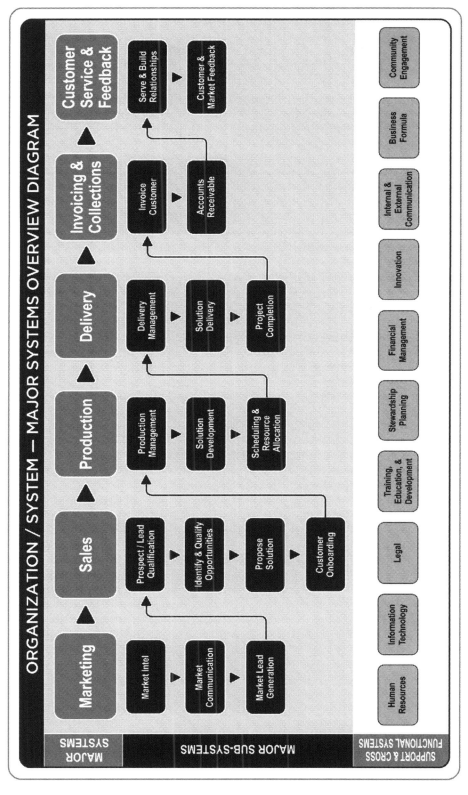

Figure 7. Example of Major Organizational Systems Overview Diagram

As we desire to optimally manage each system identified in the organizational system overview diagram above (and value the people working in the system), we apply Managing Systems concepts. Therefore, we begin with each system (or at least prioritize the most critical systems) having its associated aim or purpose statement. Much as we begin the Board-level conversation with an Ends Policy or statement, and an organizational conversation with its Charter, we begin the systems conversation with the system's purpose. Said a different way, the purpose statement at the systems level is relatively synonymous with a Charter statement at the organization level and an ends statement at the Board level. Why? Because, as we have stated many times thus far, an organization is a system. Or better said, an organization is an organized system of systems. Why are we stating this information again? It is important that leaders of Good Place organizations understand the alignment, connection, and coherence of *The 10 Areas of Stewarding a Good Place Organization* and how to appropriately apply these methods and tools at applicable levels and contexts of the organization because they are the foundational building blocks of building a Good Place organization.

As we apply the concept of purpose to Managing Systems, you are welcome to reread the section on *Charter* to make the connection, as the following application of the topic of purpose is very similar and at times completely redundant.

(NOTE: Many system problems can be addressed right here. Many times, we experience problems because we have not clearly defined the purpose or aim, or we have not clearly communicated it, or it is not clearly understood. We may also have a lack of buy-in or commitment to it.)

As illustrated earlier in the sections on *Charter* and *Governance Leadership*, the concepts illustrated in figure 8 are also applied to Managing Systems, where we discuss systems as the means of accomplishing the purpose of the system (the ends) and we monitor the Key Outcomes and Results the system is producing as indicators of the system fulfilling its purpose.

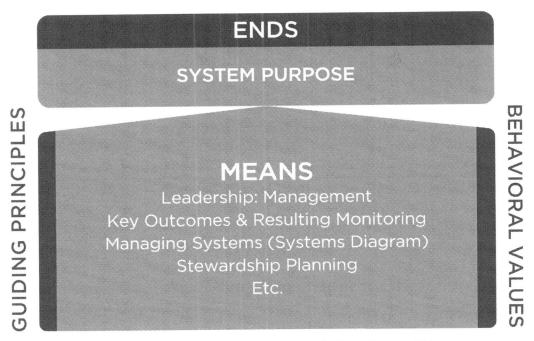

Figure 8. System Ends/Purpose, Means, and Guiding Principles/Values

Determining the Purpose of the System

Every system should have an aim, a purpose statement leading and guiding it. Examples of purpose statements for many of the typical major organizational systems are provided at the end of this section. Just as we walked through in the *Charter* section, we determine a purpose statement for a specific system by answering a few questions like the following:

- Why does this system exist?
- To what ends does this system exist?
- What difference and/or contribution does this system make in the organization?
- What is this system to achieve?
- What unique benefits does this system provide and for whom?
- How does this system align with and help fulfill the Charter of the organization?
- Who should be interested in joining and working in this system?

We then refine those ideas into a purpose statement addressing the necessary elements of a purpose and ensuring clear and compelling communication with our internal audience.

We often use the following to determine if we are addressing the baseline elements of a purpose statement:

The purpose of *THE SYSTEM* is to provide *THESE BENEFICIARIES* with *THESE BENEFITS* within *THESE GUIDING PRINCIPLES/BEHAVIORAL VALUES* commensurate with *THIS INVESTMENT/COST.*

Certainly, the purpose can be worded differently, but the statement above does a nice job of addressing the basics and does so with the Beneficiaries and their associated Benefits at the forefront.

When constructing or evaluating a system purpose, we can start with identifying the *beneficiaries*. The beneficiaries of the system can be anyone or anything that benefits from, or receives the benefits of, interacting with, engaging with, experiencing, or being a part of the system, including but not limited to its products, services, offerings, and culture. Beneficiaries can be both external and internal to the system. This certainly and most commonly includes those external to the system (depending on what kind of system it is) such as customers, the marketplace, students, etc. It could also include other things external to the system such as vendors, suppliers, the community, our planet, and creation. Beneficiaries can also include those internal to the system (depending on what kind of system it is) who work in the system such as employees, members, volunteers, contractors, etc.

The *benefits* are not features or product or service offerings, but the value provided by those things to the beneficiaries. What is the value the beneficiaries are receiving through the experience of interacting with, engaging with, or being a part of this system? When constructing or testing a system purpose, we can list the benefits each beneficiary should receive.

The *guiding principles* or *behavioral values* are the non-negotiables of how one will behave in the organization and the system within which one works. These are the values of how people agree to interact with one another, the approach they agree to take in their work and while working in the organization. In a Good Place, these guiding principles/ behavioral values are derived from the Bible, which has much to say about how we live in this world, how we view and interact with one another, how we view and interact with the world around us, how we view and interact in our work, and how we perceive ourselves in all of these interactions. Some organizations prefer to list these values separately from the purpose and vision portion of the Charter and/or system purpose. That is completely fine. The idea is that the organization has these values, clearly communicates them so that people understand, and monitors their application and engagement as a key component to building Good Place culture.

The *Investment* or *Cost* component of this statement simply reflects the financial or overall resource cost that is acceptable to provide the benefits to beneficiaries. In a Good Place organization, the cost and/or investment aligns with being a good steward of those resources in order to generate a commensurate return and to support and/or deliver economic regeneration, viability, sustainability, and/or a surplus to reinvest.

Examples of Purpose Statements

Marketing

The purpose of Marketing is to connect our organization to prospects, customers, and the community by providing actionable market intelligence to the organization; accurately positioning and building loyalty to our brand in the market, with customers and in the community; and generating interest and engagement to support our aims with new and existing markets and customers at a cost commensurate with sales and revenue.

Sales/Development

The purpose of Sales is to contribute to the understanding of new and existing markets, to identify and qualify customer needs and opportunities in those markets, to assist in providing solutions to help customers get from where they are to where they need/want to be by connecting them to our value and solutions, and to grow long-term relationships with target customers and industry contacts at a cost of sales commensurate with revenue.

Operations

The purpose of Operations is to understand new and existing markets and customers and their needs, develop and deliver new and existing value-add products to meet those needs, and help customers get from where they are to where they need/want to be in a timely, cost-effective, and high-quality manner, at a cost commensurate with market pricing and that supports the aim of economic regeneration.

Finance

The purpose of Finance is to provide organizational leaders with accurate and compliant accounting of the finances and assets of the organization, analysis, and improvement recommendations in order to make wise business decisions, and to provide training regarding the financial impact of decisions.

The purpose statements for each of *The 10 Areas* systems can be found in their respective sections of this book.

Monitor, Learn, and Improve to Fulfill the Purpose: Key Outcomes and Results Dashboard

(NOTE: This section of Key Outcomes and Results parallels the same section in the area of Charter and will be redundant intentionally, since an organization is an overall system, or more appropriately, an organized system of systems.)

Once the purpose of the system is determined, how do we know if the system is fulfilling its purpose? How do we know if we are accomplishing the purpose for which the system exists? To answer these questions, we need not look any further than the purpose statement itself for the clues and the operative words we should be focusing on to indicate if we are indeed fulfilling the system's purpose.

We identify these operative words from the purpose as Key Outcomes. How we measure or observe Key Outcomes, we call Results. Results can be measured or observed quantitatively or qualitatively and can be financial or non-financial. In short, Results are what the organization is producing and indicate successful achievement in the Key Outcome categories as defined by the purpose. Said another way, this is a way to define success and monitor key success criteria. Key Outcomes and Results go by many names, including key performance indicators, success criteria, organizational key results, objectives, and key results.

A word of warning (again): Do not confuse Key Outcomes and Results with activities. Key Outcomes and Results are ends achieved or outputs produced. They are not means performed, activities finished, tasks done, or projects completed. This is probably the most significant distinction and, in our experience, the most challenging. For some reason, we want Outcomes to be the completion of a task or project. Completing tasks and projects on time and on budget is very important, but unfortunately, we can complete tasks and not produce the expected Results for which the task was supposed to accomplish.

We then use the Key Outcomes and Results and build a dashboard report to monitor their achievement, the performance of the system as it relates to the fulfillment of its purpose.

In order to monitor the system's performance and tell the story of how the system is performing in fulfilling its purpose, we include specific data and informational elements in a Key Outcomes and Results Dashboard or report (figure 9).

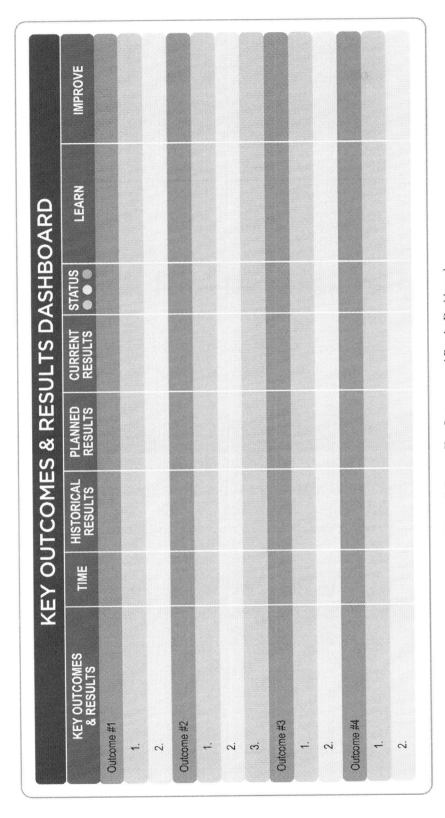

Figure 9. System Key Outcomes and Results Dashboard

Definitions of Key Terms

System Purpose: "The Words at the Top," the purpose of the system. This is very similar to the Charter we discussed earlier since an organization is an organized system of systems.

Key Outcomes: Operative words from the purpose; key categories in which we should measure or observe results to determine purpose fulfillment.

Results: Reasonable (and brief) descriptions of the measurable or observable, quantitative or qualitative data indicators that indicate the achievement of an Outcome. There may be multiple Results to indicate achievement in one Outcome. These may be financial or non-financial. Results are ideally described in terms of or include a unit of measure.

The following information should be provided for each Result:

Time: The timeframe to achieve and/or update Results—monthly, quarterly, annually, year-to-date, due date, etc. We can use multiple timeframes to track our Results in order to effectively tell the story of performance and achievement.

Historical Results: The Results data the system has historically produced in the defined timeframe(s). Results data is ideally recorded as a quantity and its associated unit of measure.

Planned Results: The discerned predicted Results data expected to be achieved in the defined timeframe(s) as determined through the impact of System Improvement(s), either stand-alone and/or thorough Stewardship Planning. Results data is ideally recorded as a quantity and its associated unit of measure.

Current Results: The Results data the system is actually and currently producing in the defined timeframe(s). Results data is ideally recorded as a quantity and its associated unit of measure.

Status: Comparison of the Current Results, the system is producing with Planned and/or Historical Results, which gives an at-a-glance indicator as to whether our performance/achievement of the Result is ON TRACK, CAUTIONARY (we need to keep a close eye on this), or OFF TRACK. We can use simple "stoplight" indicators—green, yellow, or red—or whatever other symbols we would like to use to indicate this.

The following information should also be provided for each Result, or at least each Result that is significantly ON or OFF TRACK, or any other issue that needs to be highlighted:

> **Learn:** The root cause(s) of why the system is producing the particular Results data. (We will talk more about "Learn" later in this section.)

> **Improve:** System Improvements—the enhancements or corrections recommended and/or implemented based on the Current Results data produced, Status, and root cause. (We will talk more about "Improve" later in this section.)

We use these informational elements of the Key Outcomes and Results Dashboard to tell a story. For each Result, we tell the following story:

- What timeframe(s) makes most sense to measure or observe these Results?

- What has the organization/system produced in the past?

- What do we intelligently predict the organization/system will produce based on our planning (see Stewardship Planning) and the impact of Strategic Initiatives or System Improvements?

- What is the organization/system currently producing in that timeframe(s)?

- Is the Current Result on track, off track, cautionary (or some other status) compared to the Planned Results and/or the Historical Results?

- Why is the organization/system producing that Current Result?

- Should we do anything about it? Should we implement an improvement, an enhancement to a system producing on-track Results, or a corrective action to a system producing off-track results?

As we previously discussed in the section on *Charter*, there are three main audiences of the information in a Key Outcomes and Results Dashboard. In this case, one is the System Manager—the person responsible and accountable for the fulfillment of the purpose of the system and the system itself. The second is the people who work in the system to understand how the organization is doing in fulfilling the purpose and achieving Key Outcomes and Results, and their valuable contribution to both. Third is the person or persons to whom the System Manager reports. This could be the leader of the organization and/or a leadership team.

Let's look at the Sales/Development purpose statement provided above and work through an example of identifying Key Outcomes and Results:

> The purpose of Sales is to contribute to the understanding of new and existing markets, to identify and qualify customer needs and opportunities in those markets, to assist in providing solutions to help customers get from where they are to where they need/want to be by connecting them to our value and solutions, and to grow long-term relationships with target customers and industry contacts at a cost of sales commensurate with revenue.

The Key Outcomes we would extrapolate from this purpose statement look like the following:

1. Understand new and existing markets
2. Identify and qualify opportunities in new and existing markets
3. Connect customers to our value and solutions
4. Grow long term relationships with customers/customer loyalty
5. Cost of sales commensurate with revenue

The next step is to determine reasonable interpretations of how we will measure and/or observe the Results in each of the Key Outcome categories. For instance, we may determine the best ways to measure the Outcomes of "Grow long term relationships with customers/customer loyalty" are by measuring and/or observing the following Results (ideally described by a unit of measure):

- Customer opportunities and stage in the sales cycle
- Number of new customers
- Number of existing customers
- Number of customers retained annually
- Customer longevity
- Customer experience survey score and/or feedback

To Manage, Learn, and Improve, we need to understand the system that produces the Key Outcomes and Results. This involves developing the system diagram and identifying and/or determining each of the informational components of the system to a level of detail that allows the System Manager to intimately understand and effectively manage how things work together to fulfill the purpose of the system and value the people working in the system, so as to not cause harm to the system or the people working in it.

Then, following the information asked for in the Key Outcomes and Results Dashboard, we "tell the story" of each Result, determining the timeframe(s) to monitor and update the Results, populating the Historical Results from the past and the Planned Results for the future (more on this in the section on *Stewardship Planning*), and updating the Current Results in those same timeframes. Then we Manage, Monitor, Learn, and Improve (see figure 10).

More about "Learn"

When monitoring Key Outcomes and Results, the most important facet is not just monitoring and comparing results but learning whether the system is producing stable and consistent or unstable and inconsistent Results, and understanding why in order to determine wise improvements. Our focus in learning is to clearly comprehend why the system is producing what it is producing, especially if it is producing a result outside expectations.

A System Manager should intimately understand the overall system and the components of the system to then understand why the system is producing what it is producing. This is simply called *root cause analysis* and is especially important when we find a Key Outcome and Result significantly outside expected averages and variation. In this case, we need to dive into the source or root cause. First, we determine where the cause is coming from, whether inside the system (a process step, activity, resource or tool, position, knowledge, skill, ability, etc.) or from outside the system, an external influencer (such as markets, customers, suppliers, competitors, economy, government, regulations, world events, etc.). Once we determine whether the cause is internal or external, we then need to determine the nature of the cause, whether it is common or a special.

If the cause is common, it means that the cause is inherent in or to the system and consistently affects every occurrence of the outcome result(s). If the cause is special, it means that the cause does not exist in the system all of the time, or it does not affect every occurrence but arises out of a special circumstance, usually external to the system.

It is wise to clearly understand if what the system is producing is outside expected averages and/or variation is coming from an internal or external cause(s), is a common cause or special cause, and if we have identified the true cause or just a symptom. It is sometimes as easy as asking the *why* question at least five times to get to the root. There are many other root cause analysis tools that can be administered to help determine the true cause.

More about "Improve"

If we learn the system is unstable, inconsistent, and/or unpredictable (i.e., produces unstable, inconsistent, or unpredictable results), the first and foremost improvement is to stabilize the system until we experience consistent and predictable results.

When the system is producing stable, consistent, and predictable results, our objective then is to simply make improvements that raise or lower the average based on the "game" we are playing. Are we bowling where a higher average is desired? Or are we golfing, where a lower average is desired? We then look to narrow the range of variation and lower the standard deviation.

If we learn that the cause of performance is common, we would then improve the system through corrective action or enhancement. If we learn that the cause is special, we would then address the unique event appropriately, but not make a permanent change to the system.

However, if we initiate a change to the system, thinking we are making an improvement, without understanding the root cause—whether it is common or special, or treating a special cause as common—we are tampering with the system. We are simply reacting without thoughtfully responding. More than likely, this will actually cause more harm than good. And one of the first rules when managing a system is "first do no harm."

If, after we Learn, we determine to implement an improvement (an enhancement to a Key Outcome and Result that is "on track" or a corrective action to a Key Outcome and Result that is "off track"), we will need to determine what to change (as informed by root cause analysis), how to change (enhance or correct), and, sometimes most importantly, when to change. We then monitor the impact of that improvement for the associated Key Outcome and Result it was intended to improve to continuously Learn and Improve. Remember, it is only an improvement when it positively impacts the Key Outcomes and Results it was intended to improve.

Therefore, at this systems level the Planning, Managing, Monitoring, Learning, and Improving process becomes circular and results in continuous stewardship, improvement and ongoing (not one-time or annual) planning. Improvements can occur throughout the year, which in turn gives greater probability of successful Plan and Outcomes and Results achievement and purpose fulfillment. In turn, when all systems are functioning in this same way, we give ourselves the greatest probability of successful overall Plan and Outcomes and Results achievement and organizational Charter fulfillment. See figure 10 below to further illustrate this concept.

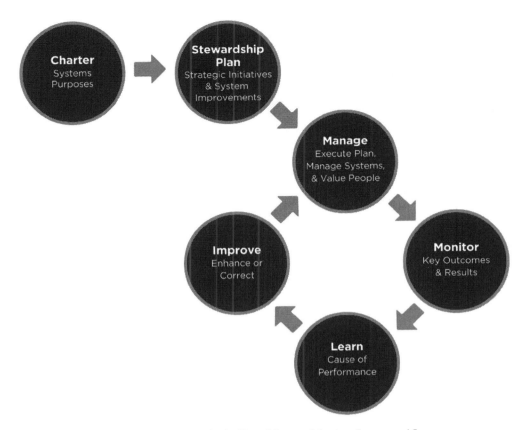

Figure 10. Stewardship Cycle: Plan, Manage, Monitor, Learn, and Improve

System Diagram and Description

We now will dive into the means by which the Key Outcomes and Results are produced and thus the purpose is fulfilled. This means is the system. The system may be described or illustrated to the level that allows for effective management of that system and valuing of the people who work in the system. We recall our mantra in this area, where our desire is to "manage systems and value people, not just manage people."

We believe that for effective systems management and valuing of people, the System Manager must be intimately knowledgeable of the people working in the system and at least the following components that make up the system in order to understand, manage, and continuously improve their system:

- System Purpose
- Key Outcomes and Results (as monitored by the Key Outcomes and Results Dashboard)
- Process Steps (first level descriptions—indicated by Roman numerals in figure 12)
- Activities (next level descriptions—indicated by capital letters in figure 12)
- Roles and Positions

- Tools and Resources
- Knowledge, Skills, and Abilities
- Feedback Loops

Which leads to:

- Job Descriptions
- Role Training
- Education
- Development

(NOTE: As we discussed earlier, Training, Education, and Development is the specific way in which we achieve the Good Place aim of valuing people.)

We could illustrate, describe, and/or document a system in many ways and to many degrees of detail. Again, the method you use depends on the information and level of detail you need to include, which depends on the purpose for which you are documenting the system.

Figure 11 is a template illustration of capturing the major system components from purpose and key outcomes to process steps through feedback loops.

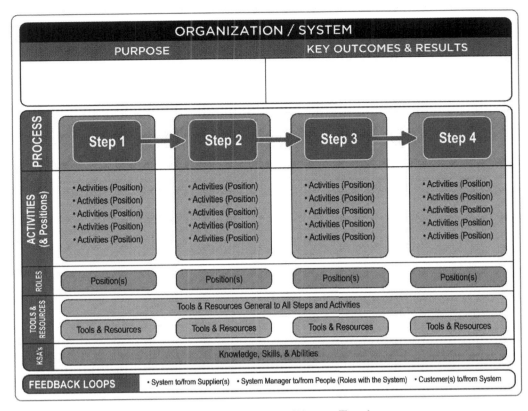

Figure 11. Overall System Diagram Template

At first glance at the illustration above, one might say it is overwhelming and too detailed. I have received this feedback. Someone else might say it is not detailed enough. I have heard this feedback as well. So which one is correct? As any good consultant would answer, "It depends." It depends on what we are trying to accomplish. Is the purpose for documenting and/or communicating the system for internal or external use, for high-level communication to new hires, or role-based training for a specific function or role within the system? The example above is mainly used for System Managers to understand their system to a level that would allow them to effectively manage the system, understanding how the system produces what it does. Therefore, it may be too detailed for external use or high-level communication to new hires. And it may be not detailed enough for specific role-based training needs.

We could also use an outline approach to document the system using Roman numerals and capital letters, where Roman numerals are synonymous with process steps and capital letters are synonymous with activities, as illustrated by figure 12.

```
┌─────────────────────────────────────────────────────────────┐
│                                                               │
│  SYSTEM:                                                      │
│                                                               │
│  PURPOSE:                                                     │
│                                                               │
│  KEY OUTCOMES & RESULTS:                                      │
│                                                               │
│                                                               │
│                                                               │
│  I. PROCESS STEP #1                                           │
│     A. Activity (Position)                                    │
│     B. Activity (Position)                                    │
│     C. Activity (Position)                                    │
│     D. Activity (Position)                                    │
│  II. PROCESS STEP #2                                          │
│     A. Activity (Position)                                    │
│     B. Activity (Position)                                    │
│     C. Activity (Position)                                    │
│     D. Activity (Position)                                    │
│  III. PROCESS STEP #3                                         │
│     A. Activity (Position)                                    │
│     B. Activity (Position)                                    │
│     C. Activity (Position)                                    │
│     D. Activity (Position)                                    │
│  IV. PROCESS STEP #4                                          │
│     A. Activity (Position)                                    │
│     B. Activity (Position)                                    │
│     C. Activity (Position)                                    │
│     D. Activity (Position)                                    │
│  Tools & Resources:                                           │
│                                                               │
│  Knowledge, Skills, & Abilities:                              │
│                                                               │
│  Feedback Loops:                                              │
│                                                               │
└─────────────────────────────────────────────────────────────┘
```

Figure 12. System Description (outline version)

What is important here is not the format we use to document but that the major components of the system are documented in a way that clearly communicates and allows the System Manager to intimately understand and effectively manage the system.

When asked the question of what level of detail we should go when documenting the system for our purpose of effectively managing the system and valuing the people working in it, the answer is twofold. First, what is the purpose for which you are documenting the system? Second, once the first question is answered, then document the system to the level of detail that allows the System Manager to understand it, effectively manage and steward it, learn from it, continuously improve it, and value the people who work in it. Therefore, the degree of detail may vary.

The following provides definition and guidance for each major system component when engaging in the exercise of documenting (diagramming or describing) a system.

Purpose

State the purpose of the system in such a way that aligns with an ends statement, which we have previously addressed and which can be clearly communicated and understood by all members of the organization.

Key Outcomes and Results

Monitor Key Outcomes and Results using the Key Outcomes and Results Dashboard concept, which allows and/or causes us to know our system, specifically what it has produced, what it should produce (through planning and improvements), what it is currently producing, how it produces it, why it produces it, what improvements to make to enhance it, and what corrections to make to fix it, allowing for continuous System Improvement as we have already addressed.

As addressed earlier, Key Outcomes and Results can be financial or non-financial in nature. The financial impact of the system is usually monitored through *Financial Management* and can include profit and loss statements, balance sheets, and/or simple monthly and annual budgets indicating financial plan to actual (and/or forecast to plan to actual).

ORGANIZATION / SYSTEM	
PURPOSE	KEY OUTCOMES & RESULTS

Figure 13. System Diagram Components Build—Purpose and Key Outcomes and Result

Process Steps

What are the critical steps needed to achieve the Outcomes and fulfill the purpose of the system? These steps are "first level" descriptions for a significant group of related activities. Process steps can also be considered subsystems as they fit the definition of a system and may require this same exercise to document in hierarchical fashion.

In Managing Systems, we generally choose to list process steps linearly and affirmatively. Meaning, for our Managing Systems purposes, we are not necessarily documenting a decision tree or flowchart with all possible yes/no decisions or if/then scenarios. In general, we document the process steps as if each is successfully achieved, the answer is "yes," and we positively move to the next step in the process.

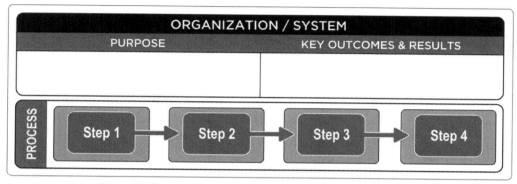

Figure 14. System Diagram Components Build—Adding Process Steps

Activities

What are the significant activities that need to be performed in order to successfully accomplish each process step? These activities are the "next level" descriptions of the individual tasks that are important to complete. At this level of detail, we need to determine if a general and brief description is sufficient to then leave the determination of the procedures to execute and complete the task up to the people working in the system. In this case a brief description is sufficient. Or the task may be deemed critical and/or needs to perform to a degree of precision and/or consistency that the procedures need to be prescribed to be done a certain way (commonly known as a Standard Operating Procedure). In this case, a more detailed description or even a separate documented procedure may be needed to describe further detail, and it may be good to indicate such on the system diagram or in the system description.

Also, if there are multiple roles/positions performing the activities (see *Roles/Positions* section below) and there are specific activities primarily performed by a specific role/position, we may want to indicate that role/position in parentheses next to the activity.

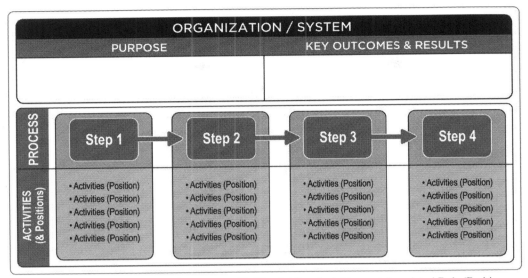

Figure 15. System Diagram Components Build—Adding Activities and Associated Role/Position

Roles/Positions

What roles or positions (depending on what you call them in your organization) are required to perform these activities? List the primary and secondary roles that are responsible for performing the listed activities according to each process step.

As just stated earlier, if there are multiple roles/positions performing the activities and there are specific activities primarily performed by a specific roles/positions, we may want to indicate that roles/positions in parentheses next to the activity.

(NOTE: The titles of these roles/positions should directly correspond to the title on their job description.)

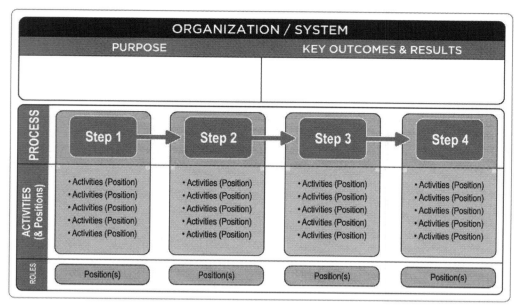

Figure 16. System Diagram Components Build—Adding Role(s)/Position(s)

Tools and Resources

What tools and/or resources are needed for the roles/positions to optimally perform the activities they are responsible for? List those that are general to the entire system and those that are specifically needed for a particular process step. These could include hardware, software applications, facilities, transportation, standard operating procedures, training documents, equipment, checklists, scripts, etc. List any significant items whose utilization lends itself to optimally performing the activities.

We can simply document these tools and resources in two categories if helpful: those that are generally used throughout the system and in every process step, and those that are only used in a specific process step.

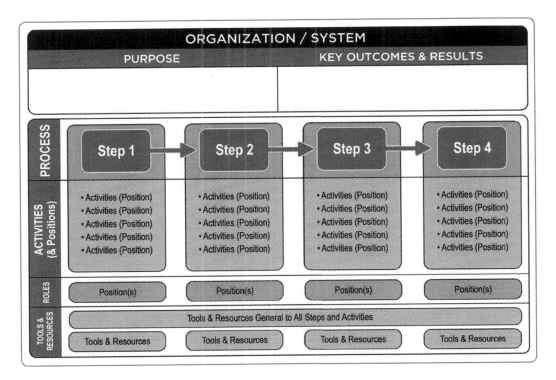

Figure 17. System Diagram Components Build—Adding Tools and Resources

Knowledge, Skills, and Abilities

What do people who have roles/positions in the system need to understand and know how to do in order to use the tools and resources to optimally perform the activities and successfully accomplish the process steps? We can identify knowledge, skills, and abilities needed to optimally work in the system in three levels. First, what knowledge, skills, and abilities does every role in the organization need? Second, what knowledge, skills, and abilities does every role in the system need? Third, what knowledge, skills, and abilities are specific to that role? The identification of the knowledge, skills, and abilities at these three levels greatly assists us in defining the training needed and developing the training matrix for each role (more on this in the *Training, Education, and Development* section).

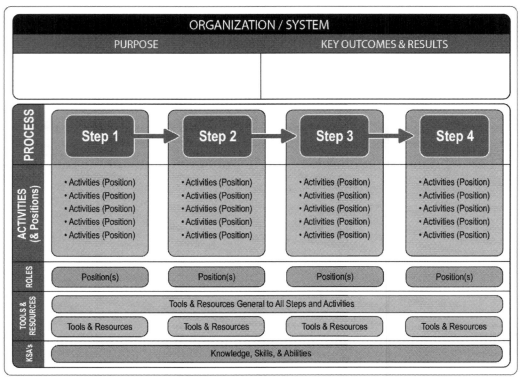

Figure 18. System Diagram Components Build—Adding Knowledge, Skills, and Abilities

Feedback Loops

The main purpose of a feedback loop is to learn information to improve the system and value people, including building trusting and collaborative relationships. There are also other purposes to consider, such as the benefit of receiving information from others whereby better decisions can be made, other perspectives are considered, etc. Also, there is the benefit of people being heard and having input into these improvements, especially if they are the recipients and/or beneficiaries of the improvement, which they usually are. This helps build trust, loyalty, collaboration, cooperation, mutual benefit, accountability, buy-in, and ownership, and it helps dispel competition.

When describing a feedback loop, we simply need to identify three main variables. The feedback formula can be explained as "X to/from Y regarding Z." Then build a system (or subsystem in this case) to accomplish the communication and information exchange that should take place between the three. We also need to ensure this is a feedback *loop* and that there is communication back and forth between X and Y regarding Z. This is not a one-way communication.

In Managing Systems effectively, we need to identify and address at least three critical feedback loops. The first is the system to and from suppliers. In this case, we need to know what is important to the system from suppliers and what is important to suppliers from the system in our relationship. What do we want or need from them? What do they want or need from us? When do we or they need it? How can we make each other better? These are important questions to answer, especially if we want to develop partnerships or covenantal-type relationships, beyond just contractual, with suppliers where we have each other's best interest in mind and desire to experience a win-win relationship by working with one another. This feedback loop can address informational topics like quality, timeliness, delivery expectations, efficiency, effectiveness, relationship, trust, integrity, communication, ease of doing business, support, training, innovation, suggested improvements, pricing, and so on. One caveat to mention here is that the reality is that not every supplier will want to enter such a dynamic, collaborative, and mutually developing relationship. This does not stop us from asking for some level of feedback from them to improve our system and continue to strive to build these types of relationships.

The second crucial feedback loop is between customers and the system. Just like with suppliers except more so, it is imperative to know what is important to customers from the system. What is important to them in our relationship? What do they want or need from us? In turn, what do we want or need from them? When do we or they need it? How can we make each other better? These questions are significantly important because we want to develop partnerships and covenantal-type relationships, beyond just contractual, with customers where we have each other's best interest in mind, desire to experience a win-win relationship by working with one another, and build up loyalty to one another. This feedback loop can also address informational topics like quality, value, timeliness, delivery expectations, efficiency, effectiveness, relationship, trust, integrity, communication, ease of doing business, support, pricing, willingness to refer, training, innovation, suggested improvements, pricing, and so on. Again, one caveat to mention here is that the reality is that not every customer will want to enter such a dynamic, collaborative, and mutually developing relationship. It does not stop us from asking for some level of feedback from them to improve our system and striving to build these types of relationships.

The third feedback loop is System Manager to/from people working within the system. In a general corporate business setting, where employees are hired to perform to generate profit as the main and/or only aim, this is traditionally known as a performance evaluation or review and is usually a one-way communication from manager to employee. While we believe sharing feedback with people is important, we also believe the traditional performance evaluation concept is lacking at best and degrading at worst, especially as it relates to the purpose of Managing Systems and valuing people to build up Good Place organizations. Therefore, in Managing Systems, we prefer the term and concept of a feedback loop. In Managing Systems, assuming we have willing workers, a worker's individual performance is really based on the system the leader has set up and determined, and the training the leader provides the worker to optimally perform their role in the system. Therefore, a traditional performance evaluation of a person is really evaluating the system the leader set up and the training the leader provided the people working in the system. Again, this approach is assuming we have willing workers (positive individual attitude) who possess the competency, capacity, and capability of performing the role (a result of our hiring process properly aligning people with a role). If we do not have willing workers, then we have another kind of issue to address altogether.

Similar to the other feedback loops we have covered, we need to ask questions like what is important to both people in this relationship? What do we want or need from them? What do they want or need from us? When do we or they need it? This feedback loop can address informational topics like purpose alignment, culture, guiding principles and values, morale, safety, health and wellness, role competency (entry level to mastery), quality of work, timeliness, delivery expectations, efficiency, effectiveness, relationship, trust, integrity, communication, support, care, training, education, development, career path, innovation, policies, and suggested improvements. Most importantly, this is a two-way conversation. The System Manager and the person have an opportunity to share their informed and evidential feedback with one another. The purpose here is still to manage and improve the system, value people, and build relationships, but it is also to support the continued building of a culture and community of care, development, and Good Place organizational life, building up hearts of love and lives of shalom.

There are a myriad of other feedback loops to consider inside and outside the system. Again, the purpose of feedback loops is to improve the system and value people. For instance, each process step in the system is a system (or perhaps better stated as a subsystem) in and of itself and, therefore, has customers and suppliers.

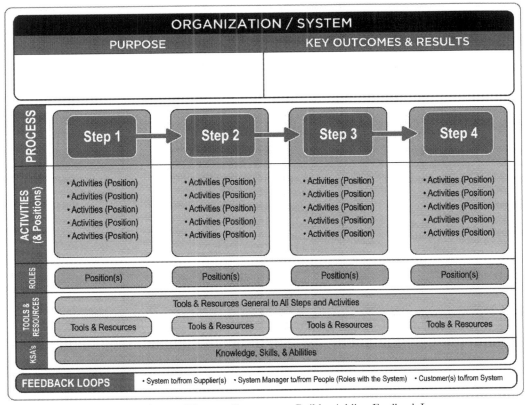

Figure 19. System Diagram Components Build—Adding Feedback Loops

Bringing It All Together—System Story and Diagram

When we put the system diagram together, as in figure 19, we get a cohesive and coherent story that works from the bottom up and goes like this: What knowledge, skills, and abilities are needed to utilize the tools and resources by people (in their roles/positions) to optimally perform the activities to successfully accomplish the process steps in order to achieve the Key Outcomes and Results to fulfill the purpose of the system?

Example of the System Diagram for the Sales/Development System

Let us take our Sales/Development example one step further from the purpose statement and Key Outcomes and Results previously illustrated, to this system diagram below, giving an example of all the system components populated, giving the System Manager an intimate understanding of the system that produces the Key Outcomes and Results that indicate fulfillment of the purpose of the system, in other words, understanding the means that produce the ends.

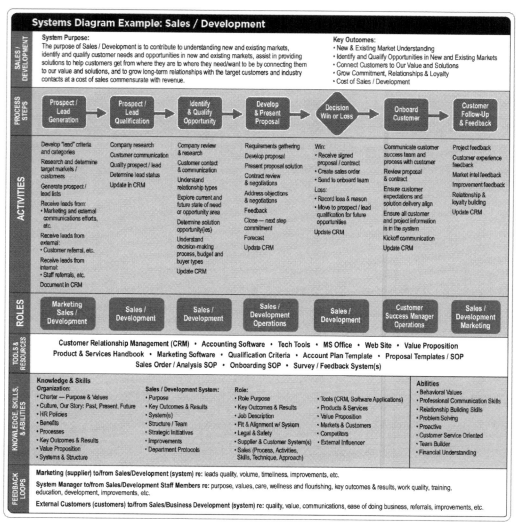

Figure 20. Example System Diagram for Sales/Development

We then use the system diagram we have documented as the foundation and information source for the developing job/position descriptions and role-based training matrix per position.

Ideally, there is a job description for every position/role identified in the system. The purpose of the job description is to communicate the purpose, responsibilities, and expectations of the position accurately, thoroughly, and clearly to help identify the training this role requires to equip and empower the person to reach their full potential and full competency in the role, and most importantly to illustrate the contribution and collective alignment to fulfilling the shared purpose of the system and Charter of the organization.

When developing a job description with this purpose in mind, we begin with identifying the general information at the top such as the position/role title (as listed in the system diagram), the department the position resides in, the status of the role (full - or part-time and exempt or non-exempt), the title of the position this position reports to, the date and version, and who approved this description.

In the body of the job description, we first state the *Charter* of the organization and then the purpose statement of the department/system the position works in and collectively aligns with to help fulfill. Then we state the purpose and summary description of the position. Next, we list key responsibilities which come from a combination of sources including the purpose of the position and the process steps and activities from the system diagram. Next, we list the knowledge, skills, and abilities needed to accomplish the key responsibilities which also come directly from the system diagram. We then list the appropriate level of education and experience needed and/or desired, which is usually directly connected to fulfilling the position purpose, performing the activities and/or utilizing the tools and resources used to perform the job. Lastly, we list the work conditions and physical demands of the job.

As mentioned earlier, the job description, along with any systems the position is a part of, are the primary information sources for identifying and developing the appropriate training for the position. We will dive into the Training subject in greater depth in the next section on *Training, Education, and Development.*

And as the system operates and we engage in feedback loops, especially at the System Manager to/from the people who work in the system, we will have ample opportunities to identify individual Education and Development considerations.

The following figure 21 illustrates how these overall Managing Systems concepts integrate and align with one another, from the overall organization to the systems that make up the organization, to the roles that work within the systems, to the training, education and development of the people that serve in those roles.

Organization
(System of Systems)

- Organization Charter
- Key Outcomes and Results Dashboard or Report
- Major Systems Diagram

Departments/ Functions
(Systems and Sub-Systems)

- System Purpose
- Key Outcomes and Results Dashboard or Report
- Systems Diagrams

Roles/ Positions

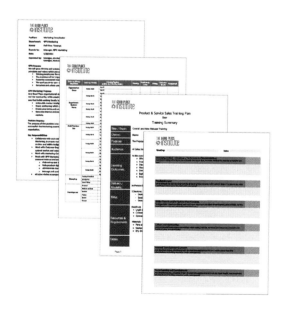

- Job Description
- Role-Training Matrix
- Training Plans
- Education Plans
- Development Plans
- Feedback Loop: Systems Manager to/from Employee

Figure 21. Organization, System, and Role Integration and Alignment

Analogy from Sport, continued

To continue our analogy from sport from the section on *Charter*, we add in the element of Managing Systems, the means. In our simple analogy we said that, along with playing with character within the rules, winning is one of the main purposes, or ends, we desire to fulfill and, therefore, a Key Outcome and Result we desire to achieve. The results are easily indicated by the points on the scoreboard and the win/loss record throughout the season. We mentioned the game plan the coach put together, which is the means the coach determines for the team to execute (and play within) in order to have the best probability of success, fulfilling the desired purpose and achieving the desired outcomes on a consistent basis. The game plan includes the plays and movements the individual players, playing their positions, are to perform. It informs what the players need to know, what they need to do, decisions they need to make, and actions they need to perform. It also informs the capabilities needed of the players, the make-up of the team, and what the team works on in practice (*Training*).

This game plan may be adjusted or improved as the coach and team monitor their performance and learn why they are performing the way they are. The team could be executing the game plan very well, yet still be losing the game. The opposite could also be true, where the team is not executing the game plan very well, yet still winning the game. This situation is usually the exception and not the rule, and I would not want to build a team or organization around that particular strategy. It is imperative then to learn why we are experiencing the results we are experiencing, and then to make the necessary adjustments to improve our results. This is also why it is imperative to not confuse outcomes and results with simply executing activities. After monitoring the results for a period of time, the coach can then implement appropriate and informed improvements at the end of a half, a game, or a season. The coach and team then go out and execute the improved game plan, monitor the results, learn, and improve.

CHAPTER 11

AREA 4: TRAINING, EDUCATION, AND DEVELOPMENT

WE VALUE PEOPLE THROUGH LOVING, HONORING, EQUIPPING, EMPOWERING, AND DEVELOPING.

All Scripture is breathed out by God and profitable for teaching, for reproof, for correction, and for training in righteousness, that the man of God may be competent, equipped for every good work.

2 Timothy 3:16–17

Biblical Summary

As we read throughout the Bible, the apex of God's creation is people. People are the only creation mentioned that are made in God's image. People are called to image God. People are also called to work (and do good works). Work is a means of grace through which we have the opportunity to image God and do what we are designed to do and fulfill our purpose to glorify God, be fruitful, grow and develop self and others into the people God designed us to become, build society and culture, and steward that which God has entrusted to the people He created.

The Bible is useful for teaching and training to be the people we are designed and intended to be, and to operate in a way that glorifies God and brings shalom to ourselves and those around us. We are designed for work, for good works, and we have the opportunity to image God in all that we do, and in and through the work that we do. We have the opportunity for work, which is a means of grace, to make us something better than we could on our own, making us into the people we can become in our work and in our lives, building up hearts of love and lives of shalom. (For further investigation regarding verses that represent the narrative or storyline of the Bible regarding this topic, see Appendix 2.)

Principles and Values

One of the three main aims of a Good Place organization is to value people. We value people in a general sense because all people are made in the image of God. Therefore, all people deserve to be honored, to be respected, and to be loved and cared for. All people have inherent value because they are persons made in the image of God and should be viewed and treated as such.

Also, in a Good Place organization we value people specifically through Training, Education, and Development. To love and care for people, we should equip and empower them to do the very best job they can do. People should experience that they and the role they play in the organization are important and valuable to the whole. Therefore, people should understand their job, the system they work in, how their job contributes to the whole of the system they work in and, in turn, the whole of the organization in terms of achieving Key Outcomes and Results and fulfilling the system purpose and ultimately the organization Charter. This is a means of communicating with and equipping people to be about the purpose of the organization, something bigger than themselves, and accomplishing something together, in an organization, that is greater than what we could accomplish individually. It means allowing work to make us into the people we can become, to live and work as God intends, building shalom in and through our work and organizational life, and ultimately to become more like Jesus, who is our model.

Practical Application for Leaders

The Training, Education, and Development functions of a Good Place organization are specifically applied systems (and one of the three aims of a Good Place organization) that serve to grow and develop the full potential of individuals both professionally and personally, to seek and allow God's continuing creation in us (our hearts) and through us (our lives) as we live and work in the world and serve each other to make it a better place. The degree to which we cultivate the growth and development of people is commensurate with the degree to which we are building up a Good Place organization.

Applying Training, Education, and Development to the people of the organization fulfills the purpose for work that came well before us, fostering and providing the atmosphere for people to learn, grow, and develop into the people they were meant to be. This concept is the specific way in which we achieve the aim of a Good Place organization that is valuing people. It also supports us in achieving the other two aims of a Good Place organization, building up Good Places and enabling the organization to be economically regenerative.

In a Good Place organization, we have specific definitions and purposes for Training, Education, and Development, which are described as follows:

Training teaches people how to do their specific job tasks, to optimally perform their role in the system.

Education is learning beyond the task-specific training. Education includes why the work is important and valuable, how it fits with other work in the organization, and how it aligns and contributes to fulfill the purpose of the system the person works in and collectively to fulfill the overall Charter of the organization.

Training and Education combined gives the person the opportunity to reach their full potential and/or be fully competent in their role, the position they have in the organization.

Development goes beyond Education to address not just what we know and do, but who we are as a person and what we can become. Development provides opportunity and encouragement for people to progress to their full potential, fulfilling what they can become, professionally and personally, in the many facets that make up a life of well-being physically, spiritually, relationally, emotionally, psychologically, educationally, vocationally, and financially.

Training, Education, and Development together fulfills the purpose for work, enables us to be economically regenerative, and supports our work to build up Good Places in our communities.

Training, Education, and Development are uniquely applied systems in a Good Place organization. Therefore, we walk through the application of Managing Systems as we have previously discussed and apply it to the concepts of Training, Education, and Development.

The Training System

As stated in previous sections, to understand if we are fulfilling the purpose of this system, we develop the associated Key Outcomes and Results Dashboard. Therefore, we extrapolate the Key Outcomes from the purpose statement(s) for Training (and Education and Development either combined or separate) and determine reasonable interpretations of how we would measure or observe the Results in each of the Key Outcome categories. Then, following the information asked for in the Key Outcomes and Results Dashboard, we "tell the story" of each Result, determining the timeframe(s) to monitor and update the Results, populating the Historical Results from the past and the Planned Results for the future, and updating the Current Results in those same timeframes. Then we Manage, Monitor, Learn, and Improve.

To Manage, Learn, and Improve, we need to understand the system that produces the Key Outcomes and Results. Therefore, this involves developing the system diagram and identifying and/or determining each of the informational components of the system to a level of detail that allows the System Manager to intimately understand and effectively manage how things work together to fulfill the purpose of the system and value the people working in the system.

An example of a summarized system diagram for *Training* is illustrated in figure 22.

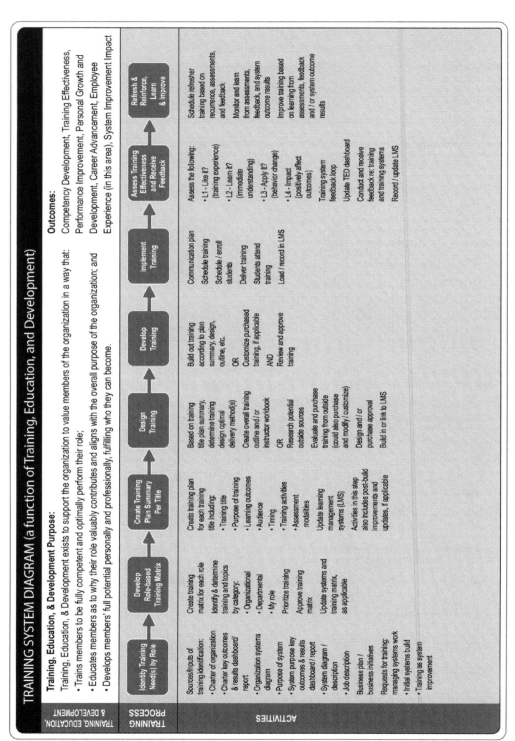

Figure 22. Training System Diagram

In managing and applying the system of Training, as illustrated above, the first process step we need to take is to identify the training needed and available in order for a person to optimally perform the tasks of the role. The information sources used to identify the training needed include the following:

- The Charter of the overall organization
- The Charter Key Outcomes and Results dashboard
- The system diagram of the overall organization
- The purpose of the system in which the role resides
- The system purpose Key Outcomes and Results dashboard
- The system diagram/description (including any supporting documents like standard operating procedures, instruction manuals, etc.) in which the role resides
- The job/position description of the role

We then document the identified training based on the information sources above and take the second process step to develop a Role-Based Training Matrix, filling out the example template in figure 23.

Training Group Alignment	Training Title(s)	Training Topics (within each Training Topic)	Priority	Proficiency Level	Timing	Delivery Mode	Completed
Organization: *Name*	*Training Title #1*	Topic #1					
		Topic #2					
	Training Title #2	Topic #1					
		Topic #2					
		Topic #3					
Department / System: *Name*	*Training Title #1*	Topic #1					
		Topic #2					
	Training Title #2	Topic #1					
		Topic #2					
	Training Title #3	Topic #1					
		Topic #2					
		Topic #3					
	Training Title #4	Topic #1					
Role/Position: *Title*	*Training Title #1*	Topic #1					
		Topic #2					
	Training Title #2	Topic #1					
		Topic #2					
		Topic #3					
	Training Title #3	Topic #1					
		Topic #2					
		Topic #3					
	Training Title #4	Topic #1					
		Topic #2					
		Topic #3					
	Training Title #5	Topic #1					
		Topic #2					
		Topic #3					
	Training Title #6	Topic #1					
		Topic #2					
		Topic #3					
Education	Coaching & Feedback						
	Learning Plan						
	Career Pathing						
Development	Vocational						
	Relational and Social						
	Emotional						
	Physical						
	Spiritual						
	Financial						

Figure 23. Role-Based Training Matrix Template

We have found the following informational elements of a Role-Based Training Matrix to be helpful:

- Training Group Alignment/Organizational Categories: This categorizes the training needed at the overall organization level, the system (department) level, and the role level. This hierarchical alignment is similar to the way we write job descriptions beginning with the Charter of the organization, then the purpose of the department/system, then the purpose of the role/position. It also is a way we can categorize the knowledge, skills, and abilities in a system diagram.

- Training Titles: This is a list of all of the training needed by title. We determine the training titles largely by referring to the documentation we listed above, which follows The 10 Areas of Stewarding a Good Place Organization, specifically Managing Systems, mainly including the system diagram of the system the role is working in. Therefore, we should expect to list Training titles like the following examples in each of the appropriate Training Groupings/ Organizational Categories:

  o Organizational Training: Charter; Key Outcomes and Results; Overall System Diagram (and how the role fits); Supplier Systems Overview; Customer Systems Overview; Feedback Loops; Overall Human Resource Policies, Benefits, etc.; Safety; and anything else all employees of the organization should know.

  o Department/System Training: System Purpose; Key Outcomes and Results; System Diagram (and how the role fits); Supplier Systems Overview, etc.; Customer Systems Overview; Feedback Loops; Safety; and anything else all employees working in the department/system should know.

  o Role/Position Training: Role Purpose; Role Job Description; Role Processes; Activities; Resources and Tools; Knowledge, Skills, and Abilities; Feedback Loops; and anything else all employees that serve in this role should know and know how to do.

- Training Topics: This lists the major topics each Training Title will address. This helps when a Training Title addresses multiple topics that are identified as needed training from the sources listed above.

- Priority: There will inevitably be a voluminous list of Training Titles for a role. This column helps prioritize training (the development and implementation of the training) and the order with which it may be scheduled to be most efficient and effective in training each person.

- Proficiency Level: This identifies the training for advancing through the beginning levels to full competency in the role—orientation, entry-level, mid-level, or full competency.

- Timing: This indicates whether the training is one-time or recurring.

- Delivery Mode: This indicates who is the lead to provide this training and the mode to be used (how it will be delivered—live, video, audio, text, hybrid, etc.).

- Completed: Progress of Training Title development as a simple way of indicating if and/or when the Training Title is ready for implementation.

Once training is identified and documented in the Role-Based Training Matrix, a Training Plan per Training Title is created. The training is then designed and developed (or purchased) and implemented. When designing the training, since training is a means to an ends (or an improvement to the means), we follow a similar course of action used when we have addressed other means topics, determining the following information in the Training Plan:

- Training Title
- Purpose of the Training
- Learning Outcomes and Results
- Audience
- Timing
- Training Activities
- Training Tools and Resources
- Feedback Loop: Assessments Modalities (to ensure and/or learn if the training and the learner are achieving the stated outcomes and fulfilling the purpose of training)

As the training is implemented, each person is then assessed as to the effectiveness of the training and the achievement of learning outcomes. As with any system, we monitor those results, learn from them, and determine improvements.

The Training Matrix should be applied to every person in that role to ensure each employee in the role has received and/or has effectively learned the training identified in their Role-Based Training Matrix and grow to be fully competent in the role. This then ensures each person in that role is fully trained, equipped, and empowered to do the best job they can do, optimally performing their role, educated as to why their role is important and valuable and how their role is aligned and significantly contributes to fulfilling the purpose of their system and the Charter of the organization.

The applicable aforementioned information should be entered into a Learning Management System, tracked, and updated per person, role, training title, etc.

Education

As mentioned above, the Education system can be managed in much the same way as Training and can be included in the Training system (and Role-Based Training Matrix) if desired. For instance, identifying the desired Education for each role follows a similar process as Training in that we identify education opportunities utilizing the same source information and can include Education Titles in the Training (and Education) Matrix. We also create the plan, design, develop, implement, assess, learn, and improve the Education in similar fashion.

We can also reach beyond a person's role to educate individuals outside of their role in anticipation of future roles and/or career path opportunities.

Since Education is learning beyond job tasks, it includes topics such as how the role the person is in and why the work they are doing is important and valuable, how the role and work fits with other work in the organization, and how it aligns and contributes to fulfill the purpose of the system the person works in and, collectively, fulfills the overall Charter of the organization. Education can also include topics that enhance the work a person does and/or topics that are transferable and/or more valuable in other roles such as the character traits of a leader (see the section on *Leadership*), critical thinking and problem-solving skills, further communication skills, learning styles, emotional intelligence, etc.

Development

Again, we utilize a Managing Systems approach to Development as we desire to develop people beyond just their role and work within the organization, to identify and make available opportunities to develop the whole person both professionally and personally. In *Develop*, our purpose is to build a culture where people are encouraged, equipped, empowered, and engaged to fulfill their potential, becoming the person they can become, flourishing and building up a heart of love and full lives of shalom. We create opportunities to develop their overall well-being not just vocationally but also physically, spiritually, relationally, emotionally, psychologically, educationally, and financially so that people can thrive and flourish as a person made in God's image, fulfilling their God-given potential, and fulfilling what they can become. In this sense, we desire to build up hearts of love and full, whole lives of shalom.

According to the Bible, the epitome and aim of our development as a person and the potential of what we can become is the person of Jesus. As image bearers of the Creator God, we are to image Him and continue to develop more and more into the likeness and image of the perfect model of humanity, which is Jesus and the principles and values of life He intends for His creation and He espoused throughout His life. Again, we desire to build up hearts of love and full, whole lives of shalom in every area of life and especially in our relationship with God, each other, and creation.

In organizational life, we desire to provide members of the organization (and perhaps their families and community) opportunities for education and development in these areas. As an example, we could use a system like the one shown in figure 24 to fulfill the purpose of Development. We can also combine this system with a development plan per individual as discussed in the System Manager to/from the person in the Managing System feedback loop.

		Vocational	Relational	Emotional	Physical	Financial	Spiritual	Community Engagement
Resources	Partners and Resources							
What We Have Now	List of **Current** Education and Development Opportunities							
What We Are Working On	List of **In-Process** Education and Development Opportunities							
Future Ideas	List of **Potential** Education and Development Opportunities							

Figure 24. Example Development System Diagram for People in the Organization

CHAPTER 11

AREA 5: STEWARDSHIP PLANNING

WE ARE CALLED TO BE STEWARDS OF ALL THAT HAS BEEN ENTRUSTED TO US.

And God blessed them. And God said to them, "Be fruitful and multiply and fill the earth and subdue it, and have dominion over the fish of the sea and over the birds of the heavens and over every living thing that moves on the earth."

Genesis 1:28

For it will be like a man going on a journey, who called his servants and entrusted to them his property.

Matthew 25:14

Biblical Summary

The Bible has much to say about planning: why we plan, how we plan, what to expect when we plan, some general guidelines around planning. There is a concept throughout the Bible that illustrates God's providence and our responsibility. He is sovereign and we are responsible. God created and owns all things, and He gives it to us to take care of and steward. This plays a significant role in our responsibility to plan and our acknowledgment that God is totally sovereign in causing or allowing all things to come about, including the outcomes of those plans.

The Bible illustrates that we have a responsibility to plan. We are to seek God's Kingdom and His purposes in those plans. We are to trust, acknowledge, and commit our plans to the Lord. We are to be guided by Biblical wisdom and discernment. We are to use good information and knowledge. We are to be unselfish, generous, and diligent; not greedy, prideful, or anxious. Lastly, we are to be good stewards of the gifts and resources we have been given to bring about a good return based on Biblical success criteria. (For further investigation regarding verses that represent the narrative or storyline of the Bible regarding this topic, see Appendix 2.)

Principles and Values

Throughout the Bible, leaders (and people in general) are called to plan, organize activities toward a purpose, and manage things under their care. We are to do all of this in the context of knowing God created and owns all things, He knows us and loves us, His ways are higher and better than our ways, He has given us gifts to be used for His glory and for our flourishing, He guides and orders our steps, and His purposes and plans are and will be victorious. Therefore, our plans should acknowledge these truths from the Bible, should bring about stewarding well that which has been entrusted to us by God, and should define success by God's economy.

Therefore, the stewardship model of planning in a Good Place organization is an organic planning approach that helps leaders steward well that which God has entrusted to them. This begins with the Charter of the organization and extends to the Plan to take strategic and tactical steps along the journey to achieve Key Outcomes and Results and fulfill the Charter within a specified timeframe. It is an approach that builds up from that with which we have been entrusted, which includes both internal and external resources, opportunities, strengths, and talents. The Plan works to answer the question: What can we build with what we have been given and improve upon what we have, directed toward achieving the aims of Good Place organizations and in alignment with the unique Charter of the organization?

We contrast this model from the predominant approach in the marketplace that builds back from financial objectives driven mainly by Wall Street success criteria and shareholders' financial expectations, as those financial objectives are at times arbitrary or mostly just expectations of monetary return by unengaged shareholders simply desiring more money from their investment.

Given our Stewardship Planning model, we believe it is always wise to begin with prayer, asking God, the Creator, Owner, and Knower of all things, to lead and guide this process of planning for the future of His organization, how to best utilize and invest His resources to take further steps along the journey of fulfilling His purpose for the organization as stated in the Charter.

Stewardship Planning also allows us to capture people's best thoughts and plot our course ahead, bringing unity to our actions and success in achieving our purpose, allowing us to coordinate resources, efforts, and thinking within groups of people working together for a common purpose. It is planning in such a way that allows investing in and developing the people and resources of the organization to continuously improve and achieving improved outcomes versus simply setting arbitrary growth targets to achieve to appease shareholders or simply adopt a cultural or Wall Street definition of success.

Stewardship Planning provides a framework (or a system), in relationship to the Charter of the organization, to understand where the organization is (the current state of things internal and external); where the organization can and/or should go from here (the future state along the journey of fulfilling its Charter); and the road map to get from current to future (or at least advancing on the road toward the future) within a specified timeframe. The framework includes the Managing Systems approach to understanding systems and improving outcomes at the overall organizational level, as well as at the level of each individual system (or department), including *The 10 Areas* systems, that are within and make up the organization, creating a comprehensive organizational plan. This approach is also designed to be continuous throughout the year versus an annual event only, to ensure room for and appropriate consideration for new information to inform adjustments and changes and to be discerning of the times, wise in decision-making to better steward the organization in its endeavors to fulfill its Charter.

It would be fair here to mention that there are many other planning models one could choose to help plan and ensure successful implementation of a plan, the achievement of objectives, and/or the completion of activities. As an example, *The Balanced Scorecard*[20] offers a planning approach from four perspectives around vision and strategy that include financial, customer, internal business process, and learning and growth. In each of these perspectives, the organization would define objectives, measures, initiatives, and actions items. Another example is planning by Objectives and Key Results (OKR's).[21] This model builds the plan through collaboratively setting goals with measurable objectives, result indicators of achieving those objectives, and the milestones needed to achieve. Yet another popular example is Traction, or The Entrepreneurial Operating System (EOS).[22] This model includes six elements including vision, data, process, traction (activities and meetings), issues, and people. Lastly, we will mention *Appreciative Inquiry*,[23] a model for organizational change focusing on strengths and appreciating the best of the organization, utilizing a 4-D model of discovery, design, deploy, and destiny.

In many of these models, and many others like them, the purpose and aims of the organization (as defined by the strategy, objectives, goals, etc.) could be anything. At best, these models are purpose agnostic, meaning they do not care what the purpose of the organization is. Generally, they are simply designed to accomplish goals or objectives by completing activities and tasks within established timeframes and budgets. Or at worst, they were consciously or unconsciously designed with a singular purpose in mind, to measure success in the most common way most businesses in the world measure it, by strictly financial measurements, maximizing revenue and profit, and increasing financial value.

This leads us to the significant differences between these many other models and the Stewardship Planning model. The differences are not necessarily the individual features of the models, as we will recognize similar (or what we may consider the best of) features found in these other models and Stewardship Planning. One of the most significant differences, as described earlier, is the approach the Stewardship Planning model takes regarding "building up" from that which currently exists and improving upon that which is currently being produced, versus "building back" from mainly financial goals. Another key differentiator is what the model is intended to accomplish and/or aiming to achieve. In the *Stewardship Planning* model, the aims are clear. We are desiring to steward well that which has been entrusted to us, building and improving upon that which has been given to us by the Creator and Owner (God), to fulfill Biblically derived success criteria, which include at least the three aims of Good Place organization (valuing people, building up more Good Places, and being economically regenerative). In addition to the unique aims for which the Stewardship Planning model has been developed and/or assembled and the features discussed previously, this is also intended to be an overall and comprehensive business and organizational planning model, uniquely aligning with *The 10 Areas*, lending itself to seamless connectivity and coherence throughout *The 10 Areas of Stewarding a Good Place Organization*.

---

20   R. Kaplan and D. Norton, *The Balanced Scorecard: Translating Strategy into Action* (Brighton, MA: Harvard Business Review Press, 1996).

21   J. Doerr, *Measure What Matters: How Google, Bono, and the Gates Foundation Rock the World with OKR's* (New York: Portfolio/Penguin, 2018).

22   G. Wickman, Traction: *Get a Grip on Your Business* (Dallas: BenBella Books, 2012).

23   D. Cooperrider and D. Whitney, Appreciative Inquiry: *A Positive Revolution in Change* (Oakland, CA: Berrett-Koehler Publishers, 2005).

Practical Application for Leaders

In Good Place organizations, Stewardship Planning is a specifically applied system that helps determine and document a road map to steward well that which has been entrusted, to move an organization from where we are, implementing initiatives and improvements, and achieving predicted outcomes and results to fulfill the systems' purposes and the organizational Charter, journeying toward an ideal future over the course of a defined timeframe. This stewardship approach benefits those leading and working in the organization. It focuses on stewarding and aligns talent, resources, and activities toward our shared aim. It provides a means to capture thoughts and ideas from people across, and even outside, the organization. It builds a road map from where we are starting to our desired destination, including the "stops" along the way. It helps bring together thinking and actions. It coordinates resources and connects efforts. It provides opportunity to innovate and improve to bring success in fulfilling our common purpose. It is a way we can further the understanding of our organizational Charter and systems' purposes and communicate how each role and person in the organization is valuable and significantly contributes to the whole. It brings clarity and unity to our past experiences, the current state of things, and an ideal future in order to chart a path forward, stewarding well all that has been entrusted to us.

As stated in previous sections, to understand if we are fulfilling the purpose of the Stewardship Planning system and how we are applying it to our organization, we can develop a Key Outcomes and Results Dashboard. Therefore, we can extrapolate the Key Outcomes from the purpose statement(s) for this system and determine reasonable interpretations of how we would measure or observe the Results in each of the Key Outcome categories. Then, following the information asked for in the Key Outcomes and Results Dashboard, we "tell the story" of each Result, determining the timeframe(s) to monitor and update the Results, populating the Historical Results from the past and the Planned Results for the future, and updating the Current Results in those same timeframes. Then, we Manage, Monitor, Learn and Improve.

To Manage, Learn, and Improve, we need to understand the system that produces the Key Outcomes and Results. This involves developing the system diagram and determining each of the informational components of the system to a level of detail that allows the System Manager to intimately understand and effectively manage how things work together to fulfill the purpose of the system and value the people working in the system.

The Stewardship Planning system includes the major process steps and activities shown in figure 25.

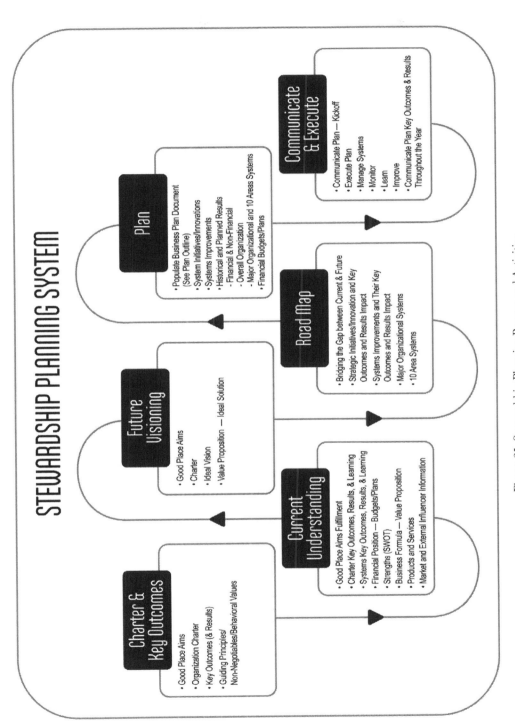

Figure 25. Stewardship Planning Process and Activities

Charter and Key Outcomes

In this step we review the items that will provide the context and direction for our plans and strategies. These include the Good Place aims, the organization Charter, Key Outcomes, guiding principles, and/or behavioral values. As always, and in particular when we are endeavoring to further determine and define means in a Plan, this step provides clarity and alignment of the common and shared purpose for which the organization exists and the non-negotiable values everyone in the organization agrees to guide behavior and decision-making.

Current Understanding

In this step we get clear understanding of the current state of things that impact the organization to know our starting point for planning. This includes considering both internal and external factors.

Internally, we clearly understand how we are doing with respect to fulfilling the overall Good Place aims and organization Charter and achieving the Key Outcomes and Results that should indicate fulfillment of both. We look at the major organizational systems and *The 10 Areas* systems that contribute to producing the organizational Key Outcomes and Results to clearly understand how each system is fulfilling its purpose and achieving its Key Outcomes and Results. We also look at how the organization is currently designed and structured.

At the overall organization level and each major systems level, we clearly understand their respective Key Outcomes and Results Dashboard, which illustrates what has historically been produced, what it was expected/predicted to be produced according to the recent Plan, what it actually produced (or currently is producing), and what we have learned as to why it has produced/performed the way it has for each Result (see Key Outcomes and Results Dashboard in the *Charter* and *Managing Systems* sections, figures 3 and 9). These should include both non-financial and financial, and could include both quantitative and qualitative, Key Outcomes and Results.

We clearly understand the financial position of the organization and of major systems. How did we perform financially according to budget, planned profitability, etc.? What is our financial position in terms of surplus resources for growth, development, investment, etc.?

Ideally, the organization is monitoring and reporting on the overall organizational Charter Key Outcomes and Results monthly, as well as each major system in the organization is monitoring and reporting monthly on their Key Outcomes and Results. Key Outcomes and Results of the individual system dashboards should directly connect and be used to populate the overall organizational Charter Key Outcomes and Results Dashboard. Collecting this information, monitoring the Results, and learning (and understanding) the root cause of performance should be in the normal course of business and not a disruptive annual event.

We build an understanding of the organization's strengths. These are those things the organization does exceptionally well, attributes that have made the organization successful. We desire to appreciate what the organization is good at. Some believe that you only need to focus and build on these strengths, capitalizing on what the organization is best at, and that will negate weaknesses. Others would desire to also consider weaknesses to solve or mitigate as well as understand opportunities and threats, more in line with a traditional SWOT analysis (Strengths, Weaknesses, Opportunities, and Threats).

We also revisit the Business Formula, specifically the Value Proposition of the organization, to review what has made the organization uniquely successful in the marketplace (more on this in the section on *Business Formula*).

We understand our current portfolio of products and/or services that deliver that value to the market and customers, and we can also dive deeper into this subject describing the current state of things such as the go-to market strategies regarding those products and services, marketing positioning, pricing, etc.

We then turn our attention to the market and other external influencers. Regarding the market and customers, we understand the current and target markets we serve in terms of direction, size, and opportunity potential as well as our market share. We also understand current and target customers in those markets in terms of personas and characteristics, need, demand, sales cycles, how they value us and our offerings, etc. Regarding external influencers, we are considering those things that could positively or negatively impact the organization and could be considered as opportunities or threats (again, in keeping with a traditional SWOT analysis). We lift our eyes up from ourselves to what is around us, the landscape of our marketplace, the horizon of the future, what is going on outside of ourselves both now and in the foreseeable future that could impact our organization. These topics include but are not limited to markets, customers, suppliers, competitors, economy, government, regulations, and world events.

Future Visioning

As we envision the future, we do so in the context and direction of the aims of Good Place organizations and the Charter of the organization. As stated previously, the Charter is the embodiment of the purpose, vision, mission, aim, values, and inspiration of the organization. The Charter is aspirational and is more of a journey to be fulfilled than a destination to arrive at, which is why we include both in the beginning of our planning discussions and in all the future-related discussions. Therefore, it only makes sense to use it to help inform and formulate a future vision.

In Future Visioning, with the aims and Charter in mind, we envision an ideal future within a foreseeable period of time—usually a multi-year ideal look. We have found that focusing on the ideal breaks us free of limitations, constraints, even practicality, and the proverbial "inside the box" thinking; and it leads to the confirmation of existing perspectives, introduction of new perspectives, identification of significant improvements, innovations, and sometimes reinvention, if necessary. It keeps us from being myopic in our thinking and gets us thinking about a bigger picture of the organization we desire to build, the business we are in, and the markets and customers we serve. In subsequent steps in the planning process we will be more realistic and practical, but while we are envisioning a future, along with our desire to innovate and perhaps even invent, we first envision and work toward an ideal without limitations, constraints, and practicality.

This sentiment is also true as we revisit the Business Formula, specifically focusing on the Value Proposition and look to update our approach and value to the marketplace. So we revisit the Value Proposition exercise (more on this in the *Managing the Business Formula* section), specifically focusing on the ideal solution in order to continue to drive innovation toward the ideal vision and/or solution to our marketplace and customer needs and opportunities.

Road Map

We know our organization's aim and Charter. We understand the current state of the organization (and how we got there) and the world around us—where we've been and where we are. We have a clear future vision and value to the marketplace—where we are going. We now need a *road map* to determine the best route to get there and/or to continue to move forward on our journey toward the future within a defined timeframe, bridging the gap between where we are and where we envision to be in the direction of fulfilling our Good Place aims and our organizational Charter, achieving Improved Key Outcomes and Results.

Our first step, then, is to identify the major activities and/or major "destinations" along our route. What are the tasks, projects, improvements, initiatives, etc. we need to address and/or accomplish to bridge the gap within the specified timeframe? What should we keep, improve, start, or stop doing? In Stewardship Planning we categories these as either Strategic Initiatives or System Improvements.

Strategic Initiatives are endeavors that are innovative, something new to the organization, like producing new things or new systems (see the section on *Managing Innovation* for further definition). Strategic Initiatives can also be large and/or strategic organizational endeavors spanning multiple departments (systems) or efforts that move the organization significantly forward in some new or disruptive way. This could mean pursuing new markets, developing and delivering new products or services, implementing new processes or systems, and the like. For each Strategic Initiative, we would ideally develop a Strategic Initiative Plan Summary (see figure 26, Strategic Initiative Plan Summary Template). As we will see while filling out the Strategic Initiative Plan Summary, there are several categories of information that will help in managing the initiative and connecting it with the Business Plan, as well as continue to perpetuate Managing Systems thinking. We will fill in purpose, Key Outcomes and Results (only this time we will be intelligently predicting what impact this initiative will have on primarily organization Key Outcomes and Results), activities, timeframes, the owner, the team, financial impact, etc.

BUSINESS PLAN

STRATEGIC INITIATIVE PLAN SUMMARY

STRATEGIC INITIATIVE: _____

OWNER(S): _____ CREATED DATE: _____

TEAM: _____ UPDATE DATE: _____

STRATEGIC INITIATIVE PURPOSE

INITIATIVE PURPOSE (& Brief Description) from Business Plan	

KEY OUTCOMES & RESULTS

KEY OUTCOMES & RESULTS from Charter Key Outcomes & Results Financial & Non-Financial	TIME	HISTORICAL RESULTS	+ RESULTS IMPACT of Initiative	= PLANNED RESULTS	CURRENT RESULTS UPDATE	STATUS ● ● ●
Outcome #1						
1.						
2.						
Outcome #2						
1.						
2.						
3.						
Outcome #3						
1.						
2.						

ACTIVITIES

ACTIVITIES Projects & Tasks to Achieve Key Outcomes & Results	OWNER	DEPARTMENTS/ TEAMS	START DATE	END DATE	STATUS ● ● ●
1.					
2.					
3.					
4.					
5.					

Figure 26a. Strategic Initiative Plan Summary Template, Page 1 of 2

FINANCIAL IMPACT

Total Sales and Revenue Impact
Indicate the SALES and REVENUE amount in the appropriate month(s) and Total/Annual.

	Jan	Feb	Mar	Apr	May	Jun	Jul	Aug	Sep	Oct	Nov	Dec	Total/Annual
Sales													
Item 1													
Item 2													
Revenue													
Item 1													
Item 2													

Total Cost Impact
Indicate the COST amount of increase or savings (as a negative number) in the appropriate month(s) and Total/Annual in terms of Direct and/or Indirect Expenses and/or Capital Expenses. Also, indicate number of HEADCOUNT increase or decrease in the month it will begin.

	Jan	Feb	Mar	Apr	May	Jun	Jul	Aug	Sep	Oct	Nov	Dec	Total/Annual
Direct Cost													
Item 1													
Item 2													
Indirect Cost													
Item 1													
Item 2													

Cap Ex													
Item 1													
Item 2													

Headcount													
Position 1													
Position 2													

UPDATES

Update & Highlights
For Significant Current Results Update, state (1) Learn: The root cause(s) of "Why" we experienced the results we did; and (2) Improve: any recommended improvements (enhancements or corrective actions).

Date #1: Text

Date #2: Text

Figure 26b. Strategic Initiative Plan Summary Template, Page 2 of 2

System Improvements make existing systems better, thus improving associated system Key Outcomes and Results. Through Managing Systems throughout the year, we know what Key Outcomes and Results our systems are producing and how and why our systems are performing the way they are. Our desire, then, is to continue to improve them throughout the year and in our Stewardship Planning process.

Remember, it is not a System Improvement unless it positively impacts Key Outcomes and Results (see Managing Systems). System Improvements either enhance a system that is performing well or correct a system that is underperforming, based on learning and understanding the root cause of why the system is performing the way it is (i.e., achieving or not achieving the system Key Outcomes and Results). See the "More about Improve" segment in the sections on *Charter* or *Managing Systems*.

The typical major organizational systems we address in Stewardship Planning include, but are not limited to:

- Marketing
- Sales (in the for-profit world) or Development (in the non-profit world)
- Operations (meaning that which produces and delivers our products and/or services)
- Human Resources
- Finance
- Legal
- Others that are critical or unique to the organization

These are commonly the major and/or critical functions needed for the optimal and proper functioning of any organization to the extent of the scale and complexity of the organization.

We then address any improvements in each of *The 10 Areas of Stewarding a Good Place Organization* as systems:

- Charter
- Leadership
- Managing Systems
- Stewardship Planning
- Training, Education, and Development
- Managing Innovation
- Financial Management
- Internal and External Communication
- Business Formula
- Community Engagement

These system areas, working together with the major organizational systems described above, build up Good Place organizations to achieve the three main aims and any other unique purposes associated with the organization.

For each System Improvement, we would ideally develop a System Improvement Plan Summary (see figure 27), Systems Improvement Plan Summary Template). While filling out the information asked for in the System Improvement Plan Summary, there are several categories of information that will help in managing the System Improvement and connecting it with the Business Plan, as well as continue to perpetuate Managing Systems thinking. We will fill in purpose, Key Outcomes and Results (only this time we will be intelligently predicting what impact this System Improvement will have on the associated System Key Outcomes and Results), activities, the owner, timeframes, financial impact, etc.

BUSINESS PLAN

SYSTEM IMPROVEMENT PLAN SUMMARY

SYSTEM: _____

SYSTEM IMPROVEMENT: _____

OWNER(S): _____ CREATED DATE: _____

TEAM: _____ UPDATE DATE: _____

IMPROVEMENT PURPOSE

IMPROVEMENT PURPOSE: (& Brief Description) from Business Plan	

KEY OUTCOMES & RESULTS

KEY OUTCOMES & RESULTS from Charter Key Outcomes & Results Financial & Non-Financial	TIME	HISTORICAL RESULTS	+ RESULTS IMPACT of Improvement	= PLANNED RESULTS	CURRENT RESULTS UPDATE	STATUS ● ● ●
Outcome #1						
1.						
2.						
Outcome #2						
1.						
2.						
3.						
Outcome #3						
1.						
2.						

ACTIVITIES

ACTIVITIES Projects & Tasks to Achieve Key Outcomes & Results	OWNER	START DATE	END DATE	STATUS ● ● ●
1.				
2.				
3.				
4.				
5.				

Figure 27a. Systems Improvement Plan Summary Template, Page 1 of 2

FINANCIAL IMPACT

Total Sales and Revenue Impact
Indicate the SALES and REVENUE amount in the appropriate month(s) and Total/Annual.

	Jan	Feb	Mar	Apr	May	Jun	Jul	Aug	Sep	Oct	Nov	Dec	Total/Annual
Sales													
Item 1													
Item 2													
Revenue													
Item 1													
Item 2													

Total Cost Impact
Indicate the COST amount of increase or savings (as a negative number) in the appropriate month(s) and Total/Annual in terms of Direct and/or Indirect Expenses and/or Capital Expenses. Also, indicate number of HEADCOUNT increase or decrease in the month it will begin.

	Jan	Feb	Mar	Apr	May	Jun	Jul	Aug	Sep	Oct	Nov	Dec	Total/Annual
Direct Cost													
Item 1													
Item 2													
Indirect Cost													
Item 1													
Item 2													

	Jan	Feb	Mar	Apr	May	Jun	Jul	Aug	Sep	Oct	Nov	Dec	Total/Annual
Cap Ex													
Item 1													
Item 2													

	Jan	Feb	Mar	Apr	May	Jun	Jul	Aug	Sep	Oct	Nov	Dec	Total/Annual
Headcount													
Position 1													
Position 2													

UPDATES

Update & Highlights
For Significant Current Results Update, state (1) Learn: The root cause(s) of "Why" we experienced the results we did; and (2) Improve: any recommended improvements (enhancements or corrective actions).

Date #1: Text

Date #2: Text

Figure 27b. Systems Improvement Plan Summary Template, Page 2 of 2

An Analogy from a House

We like to use the following analogy to clarify what we mean by a Strategic Initiative versus a System Improvement. In our homes, we usually have everyday tasks that need to be accomplished for optimal and proper functioning (and thriving and flourishing) of our home life in the house we live in. Depending on where you live, these are things like making meals, washing dishes, mowing the lawn, doing the laundry, and the like. There are ways that we can improve these everyday tasks to have our house operate better, more efficiently, or more effectively. We could make meals ahead of time, wash dishes in a way that makes putting them away easier, use a larger machine to mow the lawn, train others in the house to do their own laundry, etc. These are System Improvements, improving the things we already do to positively impact our home life and living in our house.

Then there are major things we might undertake because of the future growth of our family or another opportunity that arises we would like to respond to in a bigger way. These could be larger activities like building another room or an addition onto the house . These are more than improvements to things we are already doing. They are larger endeavors to respond to circumstances that arise or take advantage of significant opportunities that are presenting themselves. These are Strategic Initiatives.

A point to remember is that while implementing a Strategic Initiative, it doesn't mean we stop the systems (or System Improvements) that are critical to the well-functioning of the everyday operation (or improving the everyday operation). We implement Strategic Initiatives while we are doing the normal everyday systems. We build the additional room on the house while we still make meals, wash dishes, mow the lawn, do the laundry, and the like.

The Plan

Now it is time to put all our work from the planning process together in writing. We will collect and assemble the information and work done in the Stewardship Planning process and exercises and begin to write the Business Plan document. The major sections of the Business Plan we will populate includes information for the Executive Summary, Overall Organization, Financial Summaries, Markets and Customers, Products and Services, Strategic Initiatives, Systems Improvements, as well as other financial reports included as attachments to the plan. The following is a section-by-section information outline for our Business Plan to act as a guide to develop and write a typical (and relatively comprehensive) Business/Organization Strategic Plan.

Business and Organization Plan Information Outline

Cover Page—Organization Name, Brand Logo, and Date

Table of Contents

Business and Organization Plan Body:

I. Executive Summary

II. Organization Information

    A. Organization Brand and Description—Creation Story (where we have been; where we are at; where we are going)

    B. The Purpose of Good Place Organizations (three aims)

    C. Organization Charter (includes purpose, vision, mission, values/guiding principles)

    D. Charter Key Outcomes and Results (Historical and Planned based on Strategic Initiatives and Systems Improvements)

    E. Three- to Five-Year Aim

    F. Annual Theme

    G. Organizational Strengths (can also include Weaknesses, Opportunities, and Threats)

    H. Overall Organizational Major System Diagram/Description

    I. High-Level Organizational Chart—functional or positional

    J. People—key roles and skills

III. Financial Position and Outlook Summary

    A. High-Level Profit and Loss summary (including headcount)—Historical, Current, and Planned (may also include the consolidated financial impact of Strategic Initiatives and Systems Improvement to demonstrate how we arrived at the Planned Financial Results)

    B. Revenue strategy – three years

    C. Investment strategy – three years

        i. Financial

        ii. Staffing

IV. Market and Customer Analysis and Strategy

    A. Current and Target Markets and Customers

        i. Descriptions and personas—and unique benefits provided aligned/ connected with Charter

        ii. Market opportunity potential—size

        iii. Stage of maturity and stability

        iv. Current market share

    B. Value Proposition—connected to each market/customer type?

        i. Problem/Opportunity?

        ii. Ideal Solution?

        iii. What is unique about us/our offerings that solve this need and/or gets customers closer to the ideal?

    C. Competitive Landscape

    D. External Influencers

    E. Go to Market Strategy Summary—messaging and medium, penetration and retention, sales, and revenue channels, etc.

V. Product and Services Offerings

    A. List and brief description of value and features, value proposition, and Charter fit

    B. Sales and Delivery Key Outcomes and Results—past, present, and plan

VI. Strategic Initiative Summary(ies) descriptions (indicate the following for each Strategic Initiative in the Plan)

    • Strategic Initiative title

    • Strategic Initiative brief purpose description and major activities

    • Organization or System Key Outcomes and Results that will be impacted by this Strategic Initiative—Historical and Planned Results (to be monitored on the Key Outcomes and Results Dashboard)

    • Attach individual Strategic Initiative Plan Summaries in Appendix 1

VII. Major Organization System Improvements and Impact

    A. Marketing

    B. Sales/Development

C. Operations

D. Business Services—HR, Finance, IT, Safety, Legal, etc.

E. Other "Major" Systems

Include the following information for each "major" organizational system listed above, as applicable:

- System Name
- System Purpose and Brief Description
- System Key Outcomes and Results—Historical and Planned based on System Improvements (to be monitored on the Key Outcomes and Results Dashboard for the associated system)
- System Diagram or Description
- System Improvements along with the following information for each Improvement:
  - o Improvement Name and Summary description(s) —Brief purpose description and major activities
  - o Key Outcomes and Results Impact (include the outcomes to be impacted and the predicted result impact and/or the planned results to be monitored on the Key Outcomes and Results Dashboard)
  - o Attach individual System Improvement Plan Summaries in Appendix 2

VIII. *The 10 Areas of Stewarding a Good Place Organization* System Improvements and Impact

A. Charter

B. Leadership

C. Managing Systems

D. Stewardship Planning

E. Training, Education, and Development

F. Financial Management

G. Managing Innovation

H. Internal and External Communication

I. Business Formula

J. Community Engagement

Include the following information for each of *The 10 Areas* systems listed above, as applicable:

- System Name
- System Purpose and Brief Description
- System Key Outcomes and Results—Historical and Planned based on System Improvements (to be monitored on the Key Outcomes and Results Dashboard for the associated system)
- System Diagram or Description
- System Improvements along with the following information for each Improvement:
  - Improvement Name and Summary description(s) —Brief purpose description and major activities
  - Key Outcomes and Results Impact (include the outcomes to be impacted and the predicted result impact and/or the planned results to be monitored on the Key Outcomes and Results Dashboard)
  - Attach individual System Improvement Plan Summaries in Appendix 2

IX. Appendices:

A. Strategic Initiative Plan Summary documents

B. Systems Improvements Plan Summary documents

C. Financial Outcomes and Budget spreadsheets—overall, per system

   i. Past, Present, and Plan Financials/Budgets

      1. P&L/Income Statement

      2. Cash Flow

      3. Balance Sheet

      4. Headcount

   ii. ROI Projections/Pro Forma Models

When we are determining and documenting Planned Results in the Business Plan outline above, whether the Planned Results are from the impact of Strategic Initiatives or System Improvements, whether they are financial or non-financial in nature, we can simply refer to Key Outcomes and Results Dashboards and/or the Strategic Initiative and/or System Improvement Plan Summaries to understand how this stewardship approach works, to understand the Key Outcomes and Results impact, to determine Planned Results, and to monitor progress and achievement throughout the year. It becomes a simple math exercise to calculate each of the Key Outcomes Planned Results for a Strategic Initiative that has been identified in the Stewardship Planning process, as illustrated in figure 28.

Figure 28. Strategic Initiative Planned Result Equation

The same math exercise is used to calculate the Planned Results for each System Improvement that has been identified through the Stewardship Planning process, as illustrated in figure 29.

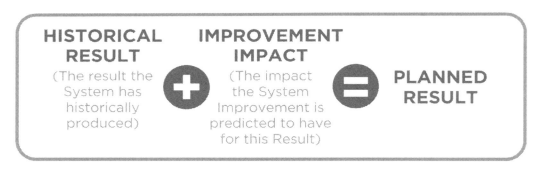

Figure 29. System Improvement Planned Result Equation

As we experienced previously, this calculation is part of filling out a Strategic Initiative Plan Summary and a System Improvement Plan Summary.

This math calculation ensures alignment with and accountability to the Key Outcomes and Results related to the Charter of the organization, the purpose of the system, and the Plan to achieve both. This type of information should be included in the Business Plan and on updated Key Outcomes and Results Dashboards (either at the organization level or systems level or both) to be monitored throughout the timeframe of the Plan and used to learn and continuously improve throughout Plan implementation.

We also apply this math calculation to financial and budget planning. What revenue, costs, profit, etc. has the organization or system produced? As we look to identify and implement Strategic Initiatives and System Improvements, what impact will they have on revenue, costs, profitability, etc.? Therefore, what should we plan on in terms of revenue, costs, profit, etc.? Once again, this information is captured in a Strategic Initiative Plan Summary and a System Improvement Plan Summary and should be consolidated across all of the Strategic Initiatives and Systems Improvements and used to produce the financial and budget plans to accompany the Business Plan.

Communicate and Execute

Once we have the Business Plan documented, the next step is to communicate it (or appropriate parts of it) to all stakeholders. These stakeholders include the leaders of the organization, those involved in Strategic Initiatives, those managing and working in the systems who will be implementing improvements, those who will be producing the Planned Results, those who will be supporting the organization in the accomplishment of the Plan and the fulfillment of the Charter. It may even include suppliers and customers of the organization, as a part of systems feedback loops, if applicable and appropriate.

We then execute the Business Plan throughout the period of time the Business Plan is intended to span. We implement the Strategic Initiatives and the System Improvements. We manage the major organizational systems and *The 10 Areas* systems. We monitor the Key Outcomes and Current Results being produced in light of the impact on results from Business Plan, Strategic Initiatives, and System Improvements that are intended to produce the expected Planned Results. We monitor on a timely basis to proact or react with wisdom and discernment in a timeframe that can be effective. We value the people in the organization by caring, equipping, empowering, and developing them. We learn and understand why we are performing the way we are, producing the results we are experiencing. We then determine if and how and when to improve the systems based on what we have learned.

Therefore, at the overall Charter and individual systems levels, as we have previously discussed, the planning, managing, monitoring, learning, and improving process becomes circular and results in continuous improvement and ongoing (not one-time, annual) planning. Adjustments can occur throughout the year, which in turn gives greater probability of successful Plan and outcomes and results achievement and Charter and purpose fulfillment. See figure 30 to illustrate this cycle and overall concept.

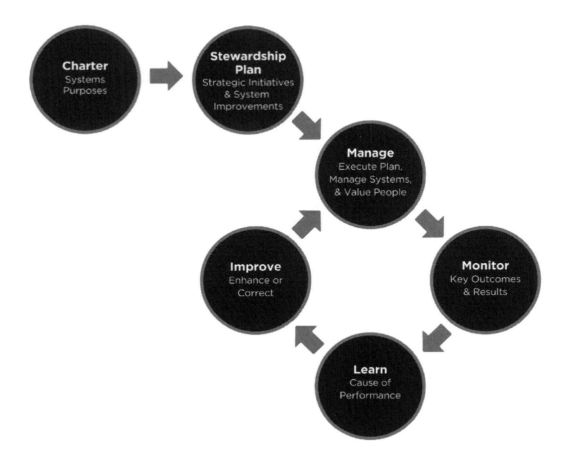

Figure 30. Stewardship Cycle: Plan, Manage, Monitor, Learn, and Improve

We want to communicate to the stakeholders throughout the year the progress of achieving our Business Plan and the monitor, learn, and improve information as appropriate for the stakeholder group. This may occur in several different communication modes and is a vital form of internal communication and feedback loop to continue to unify, value, equip, inspire, and empower the people of the organization as well as gain vital input and improvement ideas. It is a tremendous way to value those outside the organization as well as a part of external communication and a feedback loop. We will touch on the topic of communication further in the section on *Managing Internal* and *External Communication*.

The Organization Leadership Meeting

One of these stakeholder groups is certainly the leadership of the organization. This communication and feedback loop routinely occurs as a monthly business meeting of leaders in the organization and/or with those who may have leadership responsibility of the organizational leaders such as a holdings company or the like. Here is an example of a monthly meeting agenda that would align with and help guide the discussion on the concepts we have discussed thus far in the book regarding the fulfillment of the Charter, achievement of Key Outcomes and Results, progress toward accomplishing the Business Plan, etc. (see figure 31.)

ORGANIZATION:

DATE:

TIME:

LOCATION:

ATTENDEES:

Meeting Kickoff	Leader	Time
Meeting Kickoff		
Charter and Key Outcomes & Results What is important for this group to know about the previous month and year-to-date? • Fulfilling the Organization Charter • Achieving Key Outcomes & Results • Discussion and Q&A — what have we **Learned** and what are we going to **Improve** (enhance, correct, etc.)?		
Business Plan: What is important for this group to know about the previous month and year-to-date? • Strategic Initiative(s) Activity Update • Systems Improvements Activity Update		
Financials: What is important for this group to know about the previous month and year-to-date? • Financial Report and Analysis regarding Plan and Actual		
External Influencers: What is going on outside our organization (in our markets, customers, competitors, government, economy, etc.) both now and in the near future that impact our business and how?		
Looking Ahead: Organization and Financial Forecast: • Key Outcomes & Results Forecast • Financial Forecasts • Strategic Initiatives Activity Forecast • System Improvements Activity Forecast • Discussion and Q&A — what have we **Learned** and what are we going to **Improve** (enhance, correct, etc.)?		
What else would you like to discuss? Top 1 or 2 topics • What is important for this group to be aware of? • What would you like input on from this group?		
Conclusion & Action Items		

Figure 31. Sample Organization Leadership Meeting Agenda

One-Page Stewardship Plan

Organizations we have worked with not only like to have all of the Plan information in a traditional Business Plan format, but they also like to have a brief one-page illustration of the Plan for quick and easy reference of the major components that make up the Business Plan as well as the progress toward Plan and Outcomes and Results achievement, and therefore Charter and systems purpose fulfillment. Therefore, we have developed the following One-Page Plan concept (figure 32). We have also added information like an organization's history, current state, and future state to round out the story: here is where we are and how we got here; here is where we are going; and here is how we are going to get there.

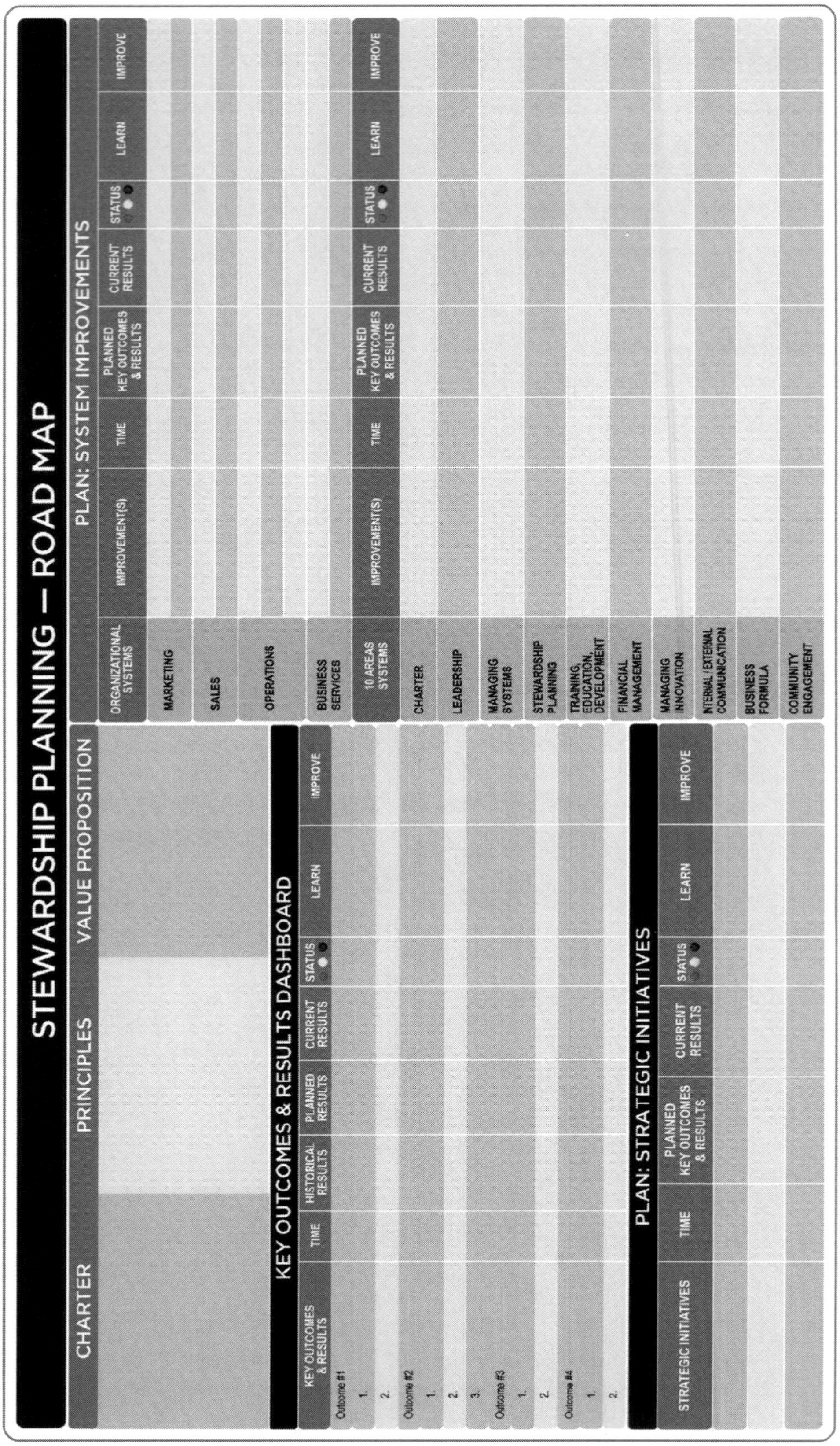

Figure 32. One-Page Stewardship Plan Example Template

CHAPTER 11

AREA 6: FINANCIAL MANAGEMENT

MONEY SERVES A PURPOSE; WE DO NOT SERVE MONEY.

No one can serve two masters, for either he will hate the one and love the other, or he will be devoted to the one and despise the other. You cannot serve God and money.

Matthew 6:24

Biblical Summary

Money is one of the most significant topics mentioned in the Bible. Some have calculated it is the second most referred to topic in the Bible with over 2,000 related verses throughout Scripture. In the Bible, we see emerging themes about money and finances. As with all created things, God is the ultimate Owner, Provider, and Giver of good gifts. We are called to steward that which He provides in a way that represents the Owner's purposes and desires for His creation. Money is no different, except money (specifically the motivation for money and for the benefits the world bestows on those who attain more of it) seems be one of those things, like power and sex, that have a tremendous pull on our hearts and seems to have a significant and unique allure for our attention and for the place of God in our lives. Many verses address the place money should have in our lives, including the purpose it serves, the motivation for it, how we attain it, and the investment and good use of it. (For further investigation regarding verses that represent the narrative or storyline of the Bible regarding this topic, see Appendix 2.)

Principles and Values

When we look throughout the Bible, we find an overall narrative regarding money and finances; we learn where finances come from, how we are to view our finances, and what finances are to be used for. We learn our finances, and all good things for that matter, come from God. They are a gift of God's grace. Therefore, we should have a proper view of finances and a healthy motivation about money. God is the Owner, and we are His stewards. He entrusts finances to us, and we are to use them for His purposes. We are to use finances to serve Him, each other, and our families and to provide for their needs and the needs of others. We are also to be wise and prudent in all our dealings and with finances.

We see these principles and values in several stories in the Bible. In the Old Testament, we see a manna economy being described where people are supplied with what they need daily to thrive, to live life, and to trust the Giver and Provider. We also see a Promised Land economy where the work that people do provides for the needs and well-being of their family and the community. We see a narrative in the New Testament where we are to be generous with our finances and joyful in our giving, and again where we provide for the needs of our family and others in the community.

Practical Application for Leaders

Financial Management is a specifically applied system that serves to accurately account for financial-related outcomes and results like revenue and expenses, ensures the use of finances are aligned with the principles stated above and the aims of the organization (namely ensuring we are generating the funds to fulfill the aims of Good Place organizations), teaches the members of the organization the financial impact of the decisions they make and the work that they do, and equips them to make wise financial stewardship decisions. Financial Management provides the financial-related data that is produced by the systems that make up the organization and, therefore, the organization as a whole, engaging with the leaders of the organization in the Managing, Monitoring, Learning, and Improving of the financially related Key Outcomes and Results of their systems.

In order to be wise and prudent in our finances and to use finances according to God's purposes and His Word, we apply financial principles and values derived from the Bible to numerous financial topics. The main topic is the overall financial condition and use of surplus resources of the organization. We call this the desire to be economically regenerative, which is one of the three main aims of a Good Place organization. This means that in a Good Place organization financial success funds the aims of the organization, which are to value people by providing work where people have opportunity and encouragement to grow and develop and where we are building up Good Places in our communities by the work that we do, making the world a better place. This also means we are good stewards of the finances and establish practices that guide the wise and Biblical use of money.

One of those applied practices is to build up a liquid cash reserve to be set at an amount commensurate with the size, cost structure, and risk-tolerance of the organization. This may mean we have liquid cash available for emergencies, to cover a certain time period of operational costs, to weather an unforeseen storm, etc. We also set the ratio of current assets to current liabilities at not less than a certain ratio, 1:1 for example. Current liabilities for this ratio will be short-term borrowing, accounts payable (trade), accrued expenses, or deferred revenue. Current assets for this ratio will be cash accounts receivables and inventory.

We consider taking wise, calculated, and good stewardship financial risks, not unnecessary risk. We invest wisely in endeavors that have high probability of yielding the type of return that fulfills the three aims of a Good Place organization. In so doing, we commit to not incur debt that could put the organization at risk. We carry no debt and/ or use debt wisely and in a manner the ensures we can pay it back in a timely manner. An example of this includes setting financial policies that include creating a debt level that is not less than a fixed charge coverage of 1.10 times at fiscal year-end on a consolidated basis. The fixed charge coverage ratio means EBITD (earnings before interest, taxes, and depreciation) divided by the sum of current maturities, plus interest expense, plus cash taxes paid, plus dividends/distributions, plus unfunded capital expenditures, plus any increase in notes receivables to related parties.

We are covenantal in our financial relationships. We will not allow financial obligations to be settled in an untimely manner, which means we pay our taxes and what is owed to our government on time. We pay our suppliers and vendors on time. We pay workers a commensurate wage for the work they do and the value they bring to the organization so that they can provide for themselves and their families.

We also establish and follow customer credit and collection policies. These policies guide our practices around the amount and timeliness of receivables to ensure positive cash flow.

Lastly, with respect to the actual, ongoing financial condition and activities, we will not cause or allow the development of fiscal jeopardy of the organization or material deviation of actual expenditures from the priorities established in the three aims of a Good Place organization and the Charter (and/or ends policies) of the organization.

In short, we desire to use finances to achieve success as God defines it in His economy, to be wise and prudent in our finances, and to use finances according to God's purposes and His Word.

As stated in previous sections, to understand if we are fulfilling the purpose of the *Financial Management* system and applying the principles and values (as described above) well, we develop the associated Key Outcomes and Results Dashboard. Therefore, we extrapolate the Key Outcomes from the purpose statement(s) for this system and determine reasonable interpretations of how we would measure or observe the Results in each of the Key Outcome categories. Then, following the information asked for in the Key Outcomes and Results Dashboard, we "tell the story" of each Result, determining the timeframe(s) to monitor and update the Results, populating the Historical Results from the past and the Planned Results for the future, and updating the Current Results in those same timeframes. Then we Manage, Monitor, Learn, and Improve.

To Manage, Learn, and Improve, we need to understand the system that produces the Key Outcomes and Results. Therefore, this involves developing the system diagram and identifying and/or determining each of the informational components of the system to a level of detail that allows the System Manager to intimately understand and effectively manage how things work together to fulfill the purpose of the system and value the people working in the system.

CHAPTER 11

AREA 7: MANAGING INNOVATION

WE BEAR THE IMAGE OF CREATIVITY AND INNOVATION.

In the beginning, God created the heavens and the earth.

Genesis 1:1

*Then God said, "Let us make man in our image, after our likeness.
And let them have dominion over the fish of the sea and over the
birds of the heavens and over the livestock and over all the earth and over every
creeping thing that creeps on the earth." So God created man in his own image,
in the image of God he created him;
male and female he created them.*

Genesis 1:26–27

Biblical Summary

In the Bible we see that God is the Creator of the world and everything in it. He is the original Creator and Innovator of new things. We see that we are made in His image and thus have been given the privilege and opportunity of co-creating and innovating as God's image bearers. (For further investigation regarding verses that represent the narrative or storyline of the Bible regarding this topic, see Appendix 2.)

Principles and Values

In the Bible we see God as Creator, and therefore, highly creative, and innovative. He created something out of nothing through His word. He created new things and new ways of doing things that had never existed before. He also created things out of that which He had originally created. He created new systems of things that work together to sustain His creation and make it flourish. This was innovative as these created things were new things and new ways of doing things to bring about the purpose of God's glory and our shalom. We see this idea of new ways of doing things and applying known things in new ways throughout the Bible, in original creation, in the new creation of peoples' lives and a place to live, in the old covenant with Israel, in the new covenant of Jesus, and many other examples. This is the definition of innovation and we, as God's image bearers through God's means of grace in life and work, are provided an opportunity to participate and experience the continuing of God's creation and innovation in us and through our activities in the world, stewarding well the creation He has provided for us to live and work, building up hearts of love and lives of shalom.

Practical Application for Leaders

In Good Place organizations, Managing Innovation is a specifically applied system that allows, encourages, and supports each person to be creative, fulfilling God's intention for us participate in continuing creation. It gives an opportunity to continually create and develop above and beyond System Improvements, which we talked about in the sections on *Managing Systems* and *Stewardship Planning* (specifically related to Strategic Initiatives). As with Training, Education, and Development, Managing Innovation helps fulfill the purpose for work, fostering and providing the atmosphere and culture for people to express and exercise their God-given creativity, as the Bible describes that all people are made in God's image and have the opportunity to image the Creator God in and through our activity in the world. This concept also inspires and allows us to achieve the aims of a Good Place organization: valuing people, building up Good Places, and the enabling the organization to be economically regenerative in new ways.

Therefore, the general purpose of Managing Innovation in a Good Place organization is to develop the system that creates ideas, develops them, and implements them, producing new things and new ways of doing things that aligns with and helps the organization better fulfill the Charter, or an organizational system better fulfill its purpose.

Furthermore, in a Good Place organization, we desire to generate, consider, and discover ideas that align with and help further fulfill the three aims of a Good Place, which lead to valuing more people, building up more Good Paces in the community, and being economically regenerative in order to sustainable accomplish the previous two. Ideally, we are looking for areas where there is a great need for shalom and/or where we could provide significant impact to building up of hearts of love and lives of shalom. Traditional approaches to innovation, especially product development, generates ideas and looks for market need, demand, or opportunity for those ideas, or they look at the market and figure out ways to meet their needs—both to sell enough products and services to make a lot of money. There is nothing wrong with an approach that discerns market need and demand to solve problems or address opportunities and make money doing it, but these are means, not ends.

To further clarify the difference between a "system improvement" and an "innovation," we can apply the following simplistic definitions. Improvements make a system better—a change to the system—in the form of enhancements to a system that is performing well and/or as expected, or a corrective action to a system that is not performing as planned and/or expected. An innovation, on the other hand, produces a better system—a change of systems—in the form of new products, services, or ways of doing things. Identifying innovations are closely tied to Stewardship Planning and usually take the form of Strategic Initiatives identified in the planning process.

As stated in previous sections, to understand if we are fulfilling the purpose of the Managing Innovation system, we develop the associated Key Outcomes and Results Dashboard. Therefore, we extrapolate the Key Outcomes from the purpose statement(s) for this system and determine reasonable interpretations of how we would measure or observe the Results in each of the Key Outcome categories. Then, following the information asked for in the Key Outcomes and Results Dashboard, we "tell the story" of each Result, determining the timeframe(s) to monitor and update the Results, populating the Historical Results from the past and the Planned Results for the future, and updating the Current Results in those same timeframes. Then we Manage, Monitor, Learn, and Improve.

To Manage, Learn, and Improve, we need to understand the system that produces the Key Outcomes and Results. Therefore, this involves developing the system diagram and identifying and/or determining each of the informational components of the system to a level of detail that allows the System Manager to intimately understand and effectively manage how things work together to fulfill the purpose of the system and value the people working in the system.

The system of innovation includes several steps and activities, which leads to decision points along the way that are intended to optimize time, effort, and resources, manage and/or minimize risk, and maximize the probability of current and future success as defined by the three aims of a Good Place organization, the purpose of Innovation and its associated Key Outcomes and Results. This systemic approach is commonly referred to as a stage-gate process, whereby we perform activities and gather information at each step in the process, then enter a decision gate at the end of that process step to determine a "go," "no go," or "go back" decision based on our findings meeting certain decision gate criteria. There are many innovation processes that follow this type of approach and generally have similar steps and activities in common. As stated in many previous sections, the system or process may not be that unique. However, the method that is chosen is determined by that which is unique, which is the purpose and aim of the system, why the system exists, and what it is meant to accomplish.

As was previously shared, Innovation can be the development of new things (products, services, businesses, etc.) or new ways of doing things. However, the following process steps, the associated activities and collected information at each step, and the decision gates at the conclusion of each step for this example Innovation system is mainly focused on the development of new things, mainly businesses or product/service offerings (see example process in figure 33).

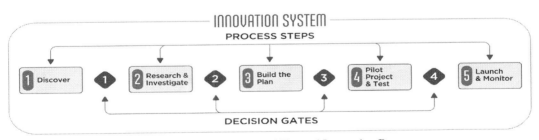

Figure 33. Example External-Focused Innovation Process

Step 1: Discover

This step generates, builds, and collects subjective and qualitative information to discover new ideas and capture as much information as we know at the time to determine if this idea meets initial criteria to take any further steps in the system and is worthy to spend substantial time, effort, and resources to pursue.

The activities and information in this step include:

1. Determine leader and team (could be both internal and external members) assigned to the development and stewardship of this innovation

2. Determine gate briefing team (Innovation steering committee who will determine gate decisions based on criteria met at each gate)

3. New business or product/service offering information

   A. Purpose and brief description

   B. Value proposition

   C. Major features and/or functionality

   D. Alignment with the overall organization Charter (or the three aims of a Good Place organization) and the purpose of Managing Innovation

4. Organization Information (what the organization has or needs related to the business and/or product idea)

   A. Charter/Purpose

   B. Key Outcomes and Result categories

   C. Three- to Five-year Aim

   D. Organizational Strengths

   E. Systems

   F. Roles and Positions, and Knowledge, Skills and Abilities

   G. Tools and Resources—technology, etc.

   H. Training, Education, and/or Development

5. Market and Customer Analysis and Strategy information

   A. Target market prospects

   B. Customer personas within each market

   C. Market opportunity potential

   D. Market maturity and stability

   E. Sales and/or revenue channels

   F. Opportunities and obstacles to market entry

   G. Competitive landscape

   H. Go to market strategy summary

6. External influencers (current or future external factors that will/may have a positive or negative impact)

    A. Markets, industry, and/or customer factors

    B. Vendor and supplier factors

    C. Competitor factors

    D. Economy and economic landscape

    E. Standards, legal, policy, and/or regulation factors

    F. Technology factors

    G. Government and/or world events

7. Business model information

    A. System requirements

    B. Human resource requirements

    C. Facility requirements

    D. Estimated financial investment

    E. Estimated Key Outcome and Result impact (financial and non-financial)

8. Identify the initial risk/reward profile

    A. Identify the risk categories from the following example considerations:

        i. Financial investment

        ii. Organizational focus

        iii. People investment

        iv. Time investment

        v. Time to market

        vi. Material/equipment investment

        vii. Legal liability and/or regulations

    B. Identify the reward categories from the following example considerations:

        i. Financial return

        ii. Organizational alignment

        iii. Market share and/or penetration

        iv. Future state achievement

        v. Efficiency

        vi. Customer Service

        vii. Pull-Through Business

        viii. Building Customer Fortresses

C. Plot an initial risk/reward position on the following example matrix

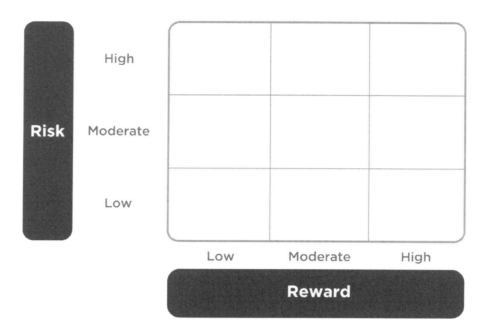

9. Probability for Success

   A. Subjective and qualitative measurement of high, medium, low

Gate 1

We use the information collected in Step 1: Discover to meet the criteria and answer the questions at this gate. The information documented in this step and gate will serve as the foundation for the gate briefing. Based on the information presented in the gate briefing, the briefing team is required to make one of three decisions: (1) Go—proceed to next step; (2) No Go—stop the pursuit of this business/product at this time; or (3) Go Back—needs more work in current step. The activities and information in this step include:

   1. Gate information and determination criteria:

      A. Is there alignment with the Charter and the purpose of Managing Innovation?

      B. Is the business and/or product and market information thorough and well thought out at this step?

      C. Does the external influencer information indicate positive and/or manageable impact?

      D. Are the business model estimates positive, attractive, and realistic?

     E. Is the position on the risk/reward profile matrix within manageable and/or tolerable risk and commensurate reward?

     F. Is the probability for success (although highly subjective at this step) medium to high?

  2. Based on the gate information, determine whether to Go, No Go, or Go Back

Step 2: Research and Investigate

In this step, we are performing research and investigation, driving at deeper and more thorough data and analytics to confirm, deny, expand, refine and/or add to the information captured in the Discover step, making what was subjective and qualitative more objective and quantitative.

1. Refine the team, if applicable

2. New business or product/service offering information

   A. Additional research and investigation to consider:

     i. Alignment with business and/or product/service offering strategy and direction

     ii. Impact considerations on current businesses or product/service offerings

3. Organization Information

   A. Additional research and investigation to consider

     i. If this is a new product/service offering, do we assimilate into the existing organization, change the organization, or construct a new organization?

4. Market Viability Information

   A. Additional research and investigation to consider:

     i. Customer journey map and customer communication touch points

     ii. Customer value and buying trends alignment with value proposition

     iii. Features and functionality fit with customer value and need/desire

     iv. Previous customer successes in similar lines of business/products

     v. Customer concentrations—geography, affinity groups, etc.

     vi. Further competitive analysis

5. External influencers

   A. Additional research and investigation to consider:

     i. Country and/or Government considerations, requirements, etc.

6. Risk/reward profile

   A. Plot new risk/reward position on the matrix

7. Probability for Success

    A. Indicate more objective and quantitative measurement from 0% to 100%

Gate 2

We use the further data and analytics information collected in Step 2: Research and Investigate to meet the criteria and answer the questions at this gate. The information documented in this step and gate will serve as the foundation for the gate briefing. Based on the information presented in the gate briefing, the briefing team is required to make one of three decisions: (1) Go—proceed to next step; (2) No Go—stop the pursuit of this business/product at this time; or (3) Go Back—needs more work in current step. The activities and information in this step include:

1. Gate information and determination criteria:

    A. Indicate the nature of the research and investigation (validating and confirming, positive or negative) and the more objective and quantifiable impact in each of the major categories analyzed.

    B. Is there continued alignment with the Charter and the purpose of Managing Innovation?

    C. Does the external influencer information continue to indicate positive and/or manageable impact?

    D. Is the position on the risk/reward profile matrix trending positively and/or still within manageable and/or tolerable risk and commensurate reward?

    E. Is the probability for success greater than 50%?

2. Based on the gate information, determination to Go, No Go, or Go Back

Step 3: Build the Plan

In this step, we build the plan that will inform and guide the launch, implementation, monitoring, learning, and improvement life cycle of the new business or product/service offering. In either case, we can refer to the *Stewardship Planning* section (specifically, the plan outline) to guide the building of a business plan or a product/service offering plan (refer to those sections that apply within the business plan). Again, in either case, the information captured in Step 1: Discover and Step 2: Research and Investigate will help populate and/or inform a majority of the information required for the plan build, with focus on determining Key Outcome and Planned Results, both financial and non-financial.

Gate 3

We use the plan developed in Step 3: Build the Plan to meet the criteria and answer the questions at this gate. The information documented in this step and gate will serve as the foundation for the gate briefing. Based on the information presented in the gate briefing, the briefing team is required to make one of three decisions: (1) Go—proceed to next step; (2) No Go—stop the pursuit of this business/product at this time; or (3) Go Back—needs more work in current step. The activities and information in this step include:

1. Gate information and determination criteria:

   A. Is there continued alignment with the Charter and the purpose of Managing Innovation?

   B. Is there acceptance of Business and/or Product/service offering plan?

   C. Is there acceptance of Key Outcomes and Results expectations?

   D. Indicate any changes to external influencer information. Does the information continue to indicate positive and/or manageable impact?

   E. Is the position on the risk/reward profile matrix trending positively and/or still within manageable and/or tolerable risk and commensurate reward?

   F. Is the probability for success greater than 75%?

2. Based on the gate information, determination to Go, No Go, or Go Back

Step 4: Pilot Project and Test

In this optional step, we may consider launching a pilot project to test our plan, including its individual components and assumptions, to learn and/or refine before a full market launch.

1. Implement Pilot Project and Test

   A. Determine appropriate Key Outcomes and Planned Results expectations of beta or test case project.

   B. Implement beta or test case in a specified sample environment that will provide learning to inform plan modifications or refinements and/or give evidence of the future success of a full market launch.

   C. Capture Key Outcome and Results data and feedback to learn and/or improve, including but not limited to the following:

      i. Customer experience feedback

      ii. Value proposition

      iii. Marketing process

      iv. Sales process

      v. Production and delivery process

      vi. Financial process and expectations

      vii. External influencers

2. Risk/reward profile

    A. Plot new risk/reward position on the matrix

3. Probability for Success

    A. Indicate more informed objective and quantitative measurement from 0% to 100%

Gate 4

We use the information and learning from this Step 4: Pilot Project and Test to meet the criteria and answer the questions at this gate. The information documented in this step and gate will serve as the foundation for the gate briefing. Based on the information presented in the gate briefing, the briefing team is required to make one of three decisions: (1) Go—proceed to next step; (2) No Go—stop the pursuit of this business/product at this time; or (3) Go Back—needs more work in current step. The activities and information in this step include:

1. Gate information and determination criteria:

    A. Was the project on time and on budget?

    B. Did the project meet or exceed Key Outcomes and Results expectations?

    C. Did Feedback and Learning indicate positive and high probability for full launch success with none to minor Improvements to the plan?

    D. Is there continued alignment with the Charter and the purpose of Managing Innovation?

    E. Indicate any changes to external influencer information. Does the information continue to indicate positive and/or manageable impact?

    F. Is the position on the risk/reward profile matrix trending positively and/or still within manageable and/or tolerable risk and commensurate reward?

    G. Is the probability for full market success still greater than 75%?

2. Based on the gate information, determination to Go, No Go, or Go Back

Step 5: Market Launch, Monitor, Learn, and Improve

In this final step, we fully implement the plan, launching the business or product/ service offering into the targeted markets. We then Manage our systems and monitor the Key Outcomes and Results they produce, learning why we are performing the way we are in the determined timeframes in order to discern Improvements. The activities and information in this step include:

1. Refine the overall Key Outcomes and Planned Results in the plan, if necessary.

2. Build out the Key Outcomes and Results Dashboard.

3. Implement completed plan to launch new business or new product/service offering to the marketplace

4. Manage systems to produce Key Outcomes and Results and fulfill Charter/ Purpose

5. Monitor Key Outcomes and Results

    A. Capture Current Results

    B. Build Historical Results

    C. Indicate Status

6. Learn

    A. Understand root cause of performance

7. Improve

    A. Enhance that which is going well

    B. Correct that which is not going well

CHAPTER 11

AREA 8: MANAGING INTERNAL AND EXTERNAL COMMUNICATION

LISTEN AND SPEAK TRUTH IN LOVE TO BUILD UP AND UNIFY.

Let no corrupting talk come out of your mouths, but only such as is good for building up,as fits the occasion, that it may give grace to those who hear.

Ephesians 4:29

Biblical Summary

In the Bible we see themes of communication such as being quick to hear and slow to speak, including being thoughtful with our words and appropriate for the audience and the situation. We also see what type of communication we should be focusing on, that communication that is truthful, loving, wise, gracious, encouraging, not harsh or rash, intentional, building up, and unifying. We should be speaking words of life versus words of death. (For further investigation regarding verses that represent the narrative or storyline of the Bible regarding this topic, see Appendix 2.)

Principles and Values

The unique thing about this topic is that the Bible itself is a communication mechanism. It is a form of the word of God. We can look at the Bible as a communication device as well as studying what the Bible says about communication to garner principles and values of organizational communication. We see the themes in these verses to focus on things that are important in communication like purpose, audience, context, method, message, and motivation.

We learn that listening is a first and significant part of any effective communication. We should listen to understand our audience, who they are, how they send and receive communication, what they need, as well as the context and the situation. We need to take time to understand these factors before we launch into speaking.

Our motivation for communication should be love, grace, and encouragement, and our words should be life-giving, building up, and unifying for the betterment and the profit of the audience and not just ourselves.

After we have listened and checked our motivation, we choose the appropriate method for communicating our message. The message, words, images, etc. we use, should be purposeful, truthful, accurate, clear, excellent, intentional, thoughtful, useful, and fit the occasion.

Practical Application for Leaders

Managing Internal and External Communication are specifically applied systems that serve to intentionally manage and optimally communicate with internal stakeholders (members of the organization) and external stakeholders (markets, customers, suppliers, community, etc.) regarding the things pertinent and interesting to that audience to build awareness, understanding, trust, healthy relationships, alignment, and influence.

The purpose of Internal Communication is to support the aims of the larger business and the business units through communication to and among our members, and to support the development of business operation/management skills through communication of business information to members. The types of communication we experience in this area can include communication regarding the Charter of the organization, the purpose of individual systems, associated Key Outcomes and Results progress and achievement, business plans, system feedback loops, policies and practices, organizational updates, etc. We can use multiple communication methods to fulfill this type of communication such as verbal (in-person and video meetings and conversations), print (business plans and newsletters), and digital (intranet sites and enterprise or collaborative applications), to cite a few examples. We can utilize all three communication methods in the training, education, and/or development of our members.

The purpose of External Communication is to build relationships among us and our external stakeholders that lead to fulfilling the aims of a Good Place organization and any additional unique aims of the organization. External Communication can also closely relate to Marketing and/or Marketing could be a vehicle to execute and/or support communication externally, especially in the form creating awareness and understanding of the organization and/or its products and services in the marketplace, brand positioning and mindshare, etc. The types of communication we experience in this area can include messaging the Charter of the organization, Key Outcomes and Results progress and achievement, business plans, system feedback loops to customers and suppliers, organizational updates, news releases, etc. We can use multiple communication methods to fulfill this type of communication such as verbal (in-person and video meetings and conversations), print (business plans and proposals), and digital (internet sites and social media platforms), to cite a few examples.

There were a few areas we have previously mentioned that also fall into this area of Internal and External Communication with the intent to fulfill the purpose stated above. We mentioned feedback loops in the section on *Managing Systems*. We also mentioned intentional communication in both *Stewardship Planning* and *Managing Innovation*, just to name a few. The point here is that the purposes of Internal and External Communication are fulfilled both through their own formally described systems and through other systems as well. We simply need to understand this system may be more cross-functional and include elements of other systems to be managed, acknowledged, and monitored through this area.

As stated in previous sections, to understand if we are fulfilling the purpose of the Internal and External Communication system(s), we develop the associated Key Outcomes and Results Dashboard. Therefore, we extrapolate the Key Outcomes from the purpose statement(s) for this system and determine reasonable interpretations of how we would measure or observe the Results in each of the Key Outcome categories. Then, following the information asked for in the Key Outcomes and Results Dashboard, we "tell the story" of each Result, determining the timeframe(s) to monitor and update the Results, populating the Historical Results from the past and the Planned Results for the future, and updating the Current Results in those same timeframes. Then we Manage, Monitor, Learn, and Improve.

To Manage, Learn, and Improve, we need to understand the system that produces the Key Outcomes and Results. This involves developing the system diagram and identifying and/or determining each of the informational components of the system to a level of detail that allows the System Manager to intimately understand and effectively manage how things work together to fulfill the purpose of the system and value the people working in the system.

As we develop the Internal and External Communication systems for our organization to fulfill Charter and purpose, we must address the aspects previously mentioned: audience, listening, motivation, methods, message, and feedback. This system, in a way, becomes circular in nature in that when we are messaging, we are also desiring a feedback loop to listen again. In listening, we ask questions to engage and understand, listening again and asking further exploratory and probing questions. In another sense, as we engage in feedback and Monitor the Key Outcomes and Results of our communication, we once again engage in Learning and Improving.

CHAPTER 11

AREA 9: MANAGING THE BUSINESS FORMULA

WE ARE UNIQUELY AND PURPOSEFULLY DESIGNED.

As each has received a gift, use it to serve one another,
as good stewards of God's varied grace.
1 Peter 4:10

Biblical Summary

In the Bible, as we experienced in previous sections, we see that God is Creator and Owner of all things. He has created all things with purpose. We see He has created the natural world to work together to fulfill His purposes. We see that as people created in God's image and through God's grace, we have been given different and unique gifts to be used for good works. We are to steward those different and unique gifts with wisdom, discernment, and according to God's ways and intentions for a life of love, peace, patience, kindness, goodness, faithfulness, gentleness, self-control, and shalom. We also see that God has established behavioral values for our good that should guide us in how we live in this world, how we view ourselves, how we view and interact with one another, how we view and interact with the world around us, and how we perceive ourselves in all these interactions. All of these many parts are to work together in unity to serve God and one another, stewarding that which He has given us to fulfill His good purposes. (For further investigation regarding verses that represent the narrative or storyline of the Bible regarding this topic, see Appendix 2.)

Principles and Values

As we read the Biblical narrative and the verses compiled to illustrate that narrative, we see themes emerge that may be viewed as a type of "formula" God uses to achieve His aims. We see God creating and organizing with purpose in mind. He creates people with different and unique gifts and resources them to steward what He has given, working together in unity to accomplish His good purposes. This is the essence of a Business Formula. As we have seen these same verses, principles, and values in other individual sections of *The 10 Areas*, we see them here collectively to develop the concept of a Business Formula where an organization is created and/or exists as a collective alignment of different and uniquely gifted people, systems, resources, etc. to steward that which has been entrusted to us to work together in an integrative way to bring value to others and to fulfill a shared purpose. In a Good Place organization, that shared purpose includes the three aims of valuing people, building up a Good Place in the community, and being economically regenerative. Therefore, we do that good work in a certain way, serving and bringing value to each other and others, and exhibiting behaviors and values that align with and reflect Biblical character.

Practical Application for Leaders

Managing the Business Formula is a way to describe and communicate to leaders of the organization the unique ways the organization creates value that pleases people, delivers the benefits of the organization to its beneficiaries, and builds loyalty to the organization. The Business Formula is an assembly of those topics that address and describe the unique ways the organization operates, delivers, and/or goes about what it does that gives a unique value in the marketplace and has made, and continues to make, the organization successful (as defined primarily by fulfilling the three aims of Good Place organizations). However, the main focus and motivation is not about advantage compared to others (i.e., competitors) but the opportunity to be co-creators, to participate with the Creator in the continuing of creation. It describes the unique essence of the value and success of the organization. It creates clarity and sustainability around the most important elements that uniquely make up the organization and what makes the organization unique and successful. And, as you will also see, the Business Formula includes, but is not limited to, several areas we have already discussed in *The 10 Areas of Stewarding a Good Place Organization*.

The Business Formula includes the assembly of answers to the following questions:

1. What are the purpose and values of the organization?
2. What unique value does the organization deliver?
3. How does the organization uniquely deliver value?

What are the purpose and values of the organization?

These subjects can be taken separately or together. Taken together, they help make up the essence of the organization's Charter which, as previously described, is the embodiment of the organization's purpose, vision, mission, aim, values, and inspiration. Clarity around the purpose of the organization, as mentioned earlier, gives direction, sets the tone, shapes culture, settles disputes, provides inspiration, brings alignment, and leads to empowerment and accountability.

The values of the organization are non-negotiable guiding principles and/or behavioral values defining how people in the organization behave no matter what products or services are provided or what markets and customers are served. These are the values of how people agree to interact with one another, the approach they agree to take in and around the work they do in the life of the organization. These are values people would not knowingly violate as an engaged and committed member of the organizational community. As mentioned earlier, some organizations prefer to list these values separately from the purpose and vision portion of the Charter. That is completely fine. The idea is that the organization has values, clearly communicates them, and monitors their application and engagement as a key component to building Good Place culture.

What unique value does the organization deliver?

In this case, we are answering the question in the context of the value the organization delivers to its customers and the marketplace. Therefore, the answer to this question is found in the organization's unique *Value Proposition,* which includes the unique strategy the organization utilizes to deliver that value.

To arrive at the answer to this question and to construct the organization's unique *Value Proposition,* we answer three important questions from the customers' perspective and experience:

1. *What is the problem we are trying to solve/opportunity we are trying to address?*
From an experiential standpoint, what problem is the customer experiencing? Or what is the customer experiencing that they may not know there could be a solution out there to better their lives, their organization, the world (i.e., an opportunity to address)?

2. *What is the ideal solution?*
Here we want to concentrate on the word *ideal.* What would be most ideal solution in the mind of the customer? Answer this question without limits, without the constraints of time, money, technology, staff capabilities, etc., describing or even illustrating the ideal experience.

This question is challenging for at least two reasons. First, some think it is a waste of time to think so far outside the box, that we should be answering it with merely practical solutions versus stretching our minds and imaginations beyond known limitations and constraints to envision ideal solutions. Second, most of us are trained formally or informally to solve problems. That is what leaders do—they fix problems. That is what the products and services of organizations do—they meet needs and fix customer problems. Both challenges are true and precisely why we ask the *ideal* question. The question forces us to innovate, and perhaps invent, versus just solve problems with practical solutions. It forces us to define our organization larger than the immediate problems we solve, needs we meet, and/or improvements to a current situation we can offer.

Staying in the realm of practical and not venturing into the realm of the ideal is the type of thinking that leads people to try to solve the proverbial problems of how to get faster horses or better railroads instead of realizing we are in the transportation business and then imagining and innovating toward better transportation. Or a global leader in camera technology trying to make better film instead of innovating better ways of capturing memories like digital or even social media platforms. Or the taxi business who kept up with small, incremental improvements, until someone envisioned a more ideal solution, innovating a new business model and disrupted an entire hundred-year-old industry. You get the idea.

With an *ideal* solution in mind, which may even be unrealistic given today's limitations and constraints, we move to the more practical and immediate answer found in question three.

3. *What is unique about the organization and how does the organization uniquely help customers get to the ideal?*
   The operative word in this question is the word *unique*. The answers to this question set the organization apart, differentiate it from others, make it special, and illustrate its unique value. It could include what is unique about what the organizations does, how it does it, why it does it, what it stands for, what has made it successful, etc.

The answers to the previous three questions form the *Value Proposition* of the organization.

How does the organization uniquely deliver the value?

The answer to this question resides overall in the aims of a Good Place organization and the application of *The 10 Areas of Stewarding a Good Place Organization*, and specifically resides in the application of Managing Systems of the organization itself. System diagrams or descriptions communicate how the organization operates, produces, and/or delivers what it was designed to produce and deliver. As we have already experienced, system diagrams or descriptions also communicate who does what, how do they it, what activities they perform, what tools and resources are used, what knowledge, skills, and abilities are necessary, etc. This systems approach captures what might be common to most organizations and what is unique to our organization. The latter is what we are specifically interested in here when we talk about the Business Formula.

The answers to the main questions above, taken and described together, constitute the *Business Formula.*

In the case of Managing the Business Formula, the Key Outcomes and Results, and the system(s) that produce those results, are for the most part addressed in other areas because Managing the Business Formula is an assembly of answers to questions already answered and/or an assembly description of areas we have previously addressed, except for the unique Value Proposition. Therefore, in order to understand if we are fulfilling the purpose of this area, we may address it individually in other areas and/or create a Key Outcomes and Results Dashboard specifically for Managing the Business Formula by assembling the data from the other areas and/or developing Results we feel are unique to this area. Then we Manage, Monitor, Learn, and Improve the Business Formula.

CHAPTER 11

AREA 10: COMMUNITY ENGAGEMENT

BUILD UP GOOD PLACES, HEARTS OF LOVE AND LIVES OF SHALOM.

Pray then like this: "Our Father in heaven, hallowed be your name.
Your kingdom come, your will be done, on earth as it is in heaven."

Matthew 6:9–10

Biblical Summary

Throughout the Bible, we see that we are called to love God and love others, and to bring God's Kingdom and those Kingdom characteristics here on earth in every sphere of life. We are given gifts and called to serve one another and pray for people's welfare, stirring each other up to love and good works, providing for each other's needs. We are God's ambassadors, representatives to model and help bring about the kind of life and experiences He intends and we were designed for.

We also see how Jesus interacts with people in the community, where He meets people in their current and humble state, serves them, meets their deepest needs, and calls and provides a way for people to experience His heart of love and His shalom. (For further investigation regarding verses that represent the narrative or storyline of the Bible regarding this topic, see Appendix 2.)

Principles and Values

Building up Good Places in the communities where we work and live is one of the three main aims of a Good Place organization. In the Bible, we see that God delegates some of the responsibility for taking care of the world to us. We are created for and to do good works that God prepared in advance for us to do. We are to seek the welfare of all peoples including those in the community where we live and work. We are to bring God's Kingdom, and the characteristics of that Kingdom, right now and right here on earth to those around us. We are to build up hearts of love and lives of shalom. We are to make the world a better place.

Through God's grace, we have all received gifts, individually and collectively. We are to use those gifts to serve one another as good stewards of those gifts. In organizations, we develop gifts, talent, skills, and abilities that serve the organization and its customers and that bring the financial return that makes the group economically regenerative. Those same gifts, talents, skills, and abilities can be applied to impact the community and make the world a better place, a Good Place.

In the Bible, we see God's original purpose for our living in the world, namely, to glorify God by living in His presence, living His way, living in and by His grace, and so participating in His continuing creation in ourselves and in the world. This is what God created us to be, to do, and to become. This is where God created us to be, to do, and to become.[24]

We also see guidance on the means to bring about this type of community. It is one of peace not violence, one of non-forcible means. Force and violence do not build up Good Places, hearts of love and lives of shalom. Superior violence may subdue inferior violence, but it does not bring about peace.[25] We see in Jesus, the Prince of Peace, our example as He committed no acts of violence against anyone. Jesus calls and provides a way for people to experience His heart of love and His shalom. We are called to an appropriate level of effort in seeking the grace that will bring God's Kingdom to our world, building up Good Places in the communities where we work and live, making the world a better place through the work we do in organizations.

Practical Application for Leaders

Community Engagement is a specifically applied system (fulfilling one of the three aims of a Good Place organization) that serves to build up Good Places in the community where we work and live by the work that the organization does, the business we are in, the products and services we provide, the skills we build up by the work that we do, and the methods and tools the organization utilizes to build up Good Places. We look into the world where there are community problems that business could solve and/ or opportunities business could address, bringing Good Place to the community where we work and live through the work that we do to earn a living. The call to build shalom and represent the Creator in creation is another purpose for our lives and our work. Intentional Community Engagement allows us to fulfill this purpose for our work and our lives in the communities where we work and live, and at times we provide this work or deliver these services even though people cannot afford to pay for it.

This is the concept behind the "non-profit dilemma,"[26] where we desire for-profit companies to take on non-profit aims of making the world a better place through the means just mentioned.

As stated in previous sections, to understand if we are fulfilling the purpose of the Community Engagement system, we develop the associated Key Outcomes and Results Dashboard. Therefore, we extrapolate the Key Outcomes from the purpose statement(s) for this system and determine reasonable interpretations of how we would measure or observe the Results in each of the Key Outcome categories.

---

24   Scott Myers, *The Eutopia Book: 1 Communities* (Tallmadge, OH: Good Place Publishing, 2017), 26.

25   Scott Myers, *The Eutopia Book: 1 Communities* (Tallmadge, OH: Good Place Publishing, 2017), 64.

26   Scott Myers, *The Eutopia Book: 0 Introduction* (Tallmadge, OH: Good Place Publishing, 2017), 56-60.

Then, following the information asked for in the Key Outcomes and Results Dashboard, we "tell the story" of each Result, determining the timeframe(s) to monitor and update the Results, populating the Historical Results from the past and the Planned Results for the future, and updating the Current Results in those same timeframes. Then we Manage, Monitor, Learn, and Improve.

In order to Manage, Learn, and Improve, we need to understand the system that produces the Key Outcomes and Results. Therefore, this involves developing the system diagram and identifying and/or determining each of the informational components of the system to a level of detail that allows the System Manager to intimately understand and effectively manage how things work together to fulfill the purpose of the system and value the people working in the system.

.

AFTERWORD

As the Founder and CEO of Kingdom Companies and former CEO of the Fellowship of Companies for Christ International (FCCI), there has been one common thread for business leaders looking to fully integrate the Bible and their faith with the leadership and operation of their company. That thread has been the question, How do I do it? How do I understand and apply what the Bible says about work, organizational life, and organizational leadership to achieve Biblical success?

While there are many books written by professional ministry leaders, there is very little written by practitioners, those who wake up every day having to balance the tension between achieving success as the world defines it, mainly maximizing profit for owners and shareholders, with success the way God and the Bible defines it. How can we make things better than we found them while building a place where those who work for us, buy from us, and sell to us can thrive and flourish? Is that even our responsibility? Or should we simply make as much money as we can, legally and morally, and give to ministries and other non-profits so they can do it?

Having been exposed to and been part of the development of these Good Place principles and practices, I am certain that they will benefit any individual and organizational leader. More importantly, when a group of leaders align to a common purpose based on a clear vision, these principles and practices are like the energy and lifeblood of that organization serving as a model of how to do it. And isn't that what we need now more than ever: proven models that can be taught, learned, experienced, and shared?

I have personally watched Scott Myers define Good Place principles, Dale Bissonette hone and apply them, and Chris Young craft them into what you have just read to be shared and learned. If you are like me, you may want to see what this is all about before you commit to the time and expense of buying and reading another book and considering another model. Let me assure you that this will be time and money well spent. This comes from someone who is wary of anyone selling another recipe or prescription for success. Every company is different, and wherever two or more are gathered, I can promise that there exists the potential for misalignment, despite the truth that God hears their prayers. Good Places do not come easily. It takes work and commitment.

This Leader's Guide is not a hypothetical treatise but rather a hands-on, practical guide that I have seen change lives and organizations for the better, including me, impacting countless numbers of others, whether employees, leaders, organizations, customers, suppliers, or the greater community at large, and achieving success as God and the Bible defines it. It has changed my perspective on how we go about Kingdom Companies.

Like any method or tool designed to change and make things better, this guide takes commitment, persistence, and practice to have any value. It is a process of change, growth, and allowing God to involve you in His continuing creation. While He rested on the seventh day, He gave us the opportunity to work, to build places of *shalom*, places where people can experience His kingdom.

Alan Ross
Founder and CEO of Kingdom Companies

APPENDIX 1

GOOD PLACE ORGANIZATIONAL
ASSESSMENT—LEADERSHIP QUESTIONNAIRE

We often utilize the following questionnaire to help assess the current state of a leader and/or an organization to help determine where we are on the journey of leading, operating, and building a Good Place organization.

Good Place Organizational Assessment

Good Place Leadership Information

		Strongly Disagree	Disagree	Agree	Strongly Agree	Do Not Know	Not Applicable
1	I am a leader who would like my organization to be a Good Place.	○	○	○	○	○	○
2	I am a leader who has the authority to determine the purpose and aims of the organization.	○	○	○	○	○	○
3	I am a leader who has the authority to determine the purpose and aims of major departmental/functional systems within the organization.	○	○	○	○	○	○
4	I am a leader who can determine the means by which those aims are accomplished.	○	○	○	○	○	○
5	I am a leader who would like to lead and operate my organization based on Good Place/Biblical principles and values.	○	○	○	○	○	○
6	I am a leader who would like my organization to have as an objective "to make the world a better place"—positively impacting individuals, communities, and creation—versus simply making money and/or giving money to others to make the world a better place.	○	○	○	○	○	○

The Three Aims of a Good Place Organization

		Strongly Disagree	Disagree	Agree	Strongly Agree	Do Not Know	Not Applicable
7	My organization is optimally functioning in and is consistently achieving **Valuing People** in a way that loves and cares for them, and that trains people to do the best job they can in their role, educates them as to why their role is important and valuably contributes and aligns with the common purpose of the organization, and provides opportunity and encouragement for them to develop their full potential both personally and professionally.	○	○	○	○	○	○
8	My organization is optimally functioning in and consistently achieving **Building Up Good Places** and having positive impacts in the community where we work and live through the products, services, work, skills, and abilities of the organization, making ourselves, those around us, and the world better.	○	○	○	○	○	○
9	My organization is optimally functioning in and is consistently achieving **Economic Regeneration**—viability, sustainability, and re-investment in growth, development, and innovation.	○	○	○	○	○	○

The 10 Areas of Stewarding a Good Place Organization:

Charter

		Strongly Disagree	Disagree	Agree	Strongly Agree	Do Not Know	Not Applicable
10	I believe God has a purpose for my organization.	○	○	○	○	○	○
11	My organization has a Charter, or the like, that embodies and/or includes purpose, vision, mission, and behavioral values/guiding principles.	○	○	○	○	○	○
12	Our Charter embodies the three aims of a Good Place organization.	○	○	○	○	○	○
13	We clearly communicate our Charter in a way that expresses the purpose for which we exist as an organization.	○	○	○	○	○	○
14	The simplest form of our Charter can easily communicate that our organization exists to deliver these benefits to these beneficiaries at this acceptable investment.	○	○	○	○	○	○
15	We have an efficient and effective way to monitor the performance of our organization fulfilling our Charter, monitoring key outcomes and result indicators (both financial and non-financial).	○	○	○	○	○	○
16	Our Charter is effectively communicated, understood, and engaged in, and all activities of the organization clearly and directly point to its fulfillment.	○	○	○	○	○	○

Leadership

		Strongly Disagree	Disagree	Agree	Strongly Agree	Do Not Know	Not Applicable
17	Our leaders clearly understand and are committed to the Charter of our organization.	○	○	○	○	○	○
18	Our leaders understand and demonstrate Biblical leadership and character.	○	○	○	○	○	○
19	I understand the difference between governance leadership and management leadership.	○	○	○	○	○	○
20	Our management leaders know how and effectively apply managing systems and valuing people.	○	○	○	○	○	○
21	Our Board functions as a policy governance board, understanding and efficiently and effectively applying the concepts of ends and means between the Board and the CEO.	○	○	○	○	○	○
22	Our Board and CEO communications and expectations are clear, delegatory, and accountable.	○	○	○	○	○	○
23	Our Board meetings are efficient and effective and focused on fulfilling the purpose (ends) of the organization within the core behavioral values (executive limitations) of the organization versus focusing on just managing the activities of the organization.	○	○	○	○	○	○

	Managing Systems	Strongly Disagree	Disagree	Agree	Strongly Agree	Do Not Know	Not Applicable
24	I am clear on what is meant by and am committed to managing systems and valuing people versus simply managing people.	○	○	○	○	○	○
25	We recognize and operate like our organization is an interconnected system of systems designed and organized to operate together to accomplish a common purpose, versus a hierarchical organization chart.	○	○	○	○	○	○
26	All our major organizational systems are identified and documented in a diagram and/or description.	○	○	○	○	○	○
27	All our major organizational systems have a clearly defined purpose.	○	○	○	○	○	○
28	We have an efficient and effective way to monitor the performance of our major organizational systems to ensure each is fulfilling their purpose, monitoring key outcomes and result indicators (both financial and non-financial).	○	○	○	○	○	○
29	We have the key components of our major organizational systems identified as: processes steps; activities; roles; tools and resources; knowledge, skills, and abilities; feedback loops; suppliers to the system; and customers of the system.	○	○	○	○	○	○
30	The purpose and description of our systems lead to and inform the job descriptions for each role in the system.	○	○	○	○	○	○
31	The purpose and description of our systems, along with job descriptions, lead to and inform the training and education of the people who work within the system.	○	○	○	○	○	○
32	We monitor key outcomes and results the system is producing to indicate whether changes we make to a system are achieving improvement.	○	○	○	○	○	○
33	We have clearly defined and effective feedback loops to and from the following three main areas to understand needs and expectations, performance, improvements, etc.: customers to/from the system; suppliers to/from system; and system manager to/from employee.	○	○	○	○	○	○

Training, Education, and Development

	Strongly Disagree	Disagree	Agree	Strongly Agree	Do Not Know	Not Applicable
34	Along with valuing people in a general sense (loving, caring for, and honoring all people), we believe that one of the best ways an organization can value a person working in the organization is by training them to be fully competent in and optimally perform their job role, educating them on why and how their role fits within the whole, and developing their full potential as the whole person they can become. ○	○	○	○	○	○
35	We have a system in place to ensure our people are trained to be fully competent and optimally perform the job roles we ask them to do. ○	○	○	○	○	○
36	We have a system in place to ensure our people are educated as to why their job role is important to the whole organization and how their job role aligns with and plays an integral role in accomplishing our common purpose, the purpose of the system they work in, and the overall Charter of the organization. ○	○	○	○	○	○
37	We use the Charter of our organization, the purpose and description of the system(s) a person works in, along with their job description to guide and inform the role-specific training and education of our people. ○	○	○	○	○	○
38	We have a system in place to ensure we are developing our people to reach their full potential as persons. ○	○	○	○	○	○
39	We have a system in place to ensure we are caring for and building up the overall well-being of our people (and their families) personally, vocationally, financially, relationally, psychologically, physically, and spiritually. ○	○	○	○	○	○

Stewardship Planning

	Strongly Disagree	Disagree	Agree	Strongly Agree	Do Not Know	Not Applicable
40	We have a planning process that is specifically designed to fulfill the Charter of our organization. ○	○	○	○	○	○
41	We have a planning process that allows stewarding, investing in, and developing the people and resources of the organization to continuously improve and achieve improved outcomes, versus simply setting arbitrary growth goals and then figuring out how to achieve them. ○	○	○	○	○	○
42	We have a planning process designed to understand the things that affect our organization, envision the future, capture everyone's best thoughts, and plot a course ahead, bringing unity to actions and success in fulfilling our Charter and achieving key outcomes and results. ○	○	○	○	○	○
43	We have a planning process designed to monitor performance to the Business Plan throughout the year, anticipate upcoming events, learn why we are performing the way we are, be aware of external influencer's on our performance, and continuously improve and adjust as necessary. ○	○	○	○	○	○

Financial Management

	Strongly Disagree	Disagree	Agree	Strongly Agree	Do Not Know	Not Applicable
44	We have an organizational system of financial management that includes accurate accounting of financials and equipping organizational leaders to understand the financial impact of the decisions they make and to make wise financial stewardship decisions, and it also includes a way of ensuring we are fulfilling these purposes, achieving key outcomes and results, understanding why we are performing the way we are, and improving continuously.	○	○	○	○	○

Managing Innovation

	Strongly Disagree	Disagree	Agree	Strongly Agree	Do Not Know	Not Applicable
45	We have an organizational system of managing innovation that encourages and supports people to be creative, think of new things to do and new ways of doing them, aligning and applying those ideas to better fulfill our Charter, and it includes a way of ensuring we are fulfilling these purposes, achieving key outcomes and results, understanding why we are performing the way we are, and improving continuously.	○	○	○	○	○

Managing Internal and External Communications

	Strongly Disagree	Disagree	Agree	Strongly Agree	Do Not Know	Not Applicable
46	We have an organizational system of managing internal communications that supports and communicates clearly and effectively the aims of the organization to the members of the organization and includes a way of ensuring we are fulfilling these purposes, achieving key outcomes and results, understanding why we are performing the way we are, and improving continuously.	○	○	○	○	○	○
47	We have an organizational system of managing external communications that supports and communicates clearly and effectively, building relationships with our external stakeholders that leads to fulfilling our Charter, and includes a way of ensuring we are fulfilling these purposes, achieving key outcomes and results, understanding why we are performing the way we are, and improving continuously.	○	○	○	○	○	○

Managing the Business Formula

		Strongly Disagree	Disagree	Agree	Strongly Agree	Do Not Know	Not Applicable
48	We have a clearly articulated and communicated value proposition answering three questions: (1) What is the problem we are trying to solve/opportunity we are trying to address? (2) What is the ideal solution? (3) What is unique about the organization, and how does the organization uniquely help customers get to the ideal?	○	○	○	○	○	○
49	The core values of the organization are clearly defined, communicated, understood, and engaged in.	○	○	○	○	○	○

Community Engagement

		Strongly Disagree	Disagree	Agree	Strongly Agree	Do Not Know	Not Applicable
50	We have an organizational system of community engagement that applies the specific skills and abilities we develop within our organization (the skills and abilities that serve the organization and its customers and brings the financial return that makes the group economically viable), to make the world (and specifically the community where we work and live) a better place.	○	○	○	○	○	○

APPENDIX 2

BIBLICAL FOUNDATION FOR EACH OF
THE 10 AREAS OF STEWARDING A GOOD PLACE ORGANIZATION

Area 1: Charter

Biblical Foundation

As you read through the Bible, and as illustrated by various verses throughout the Bible, it is clear the Bible describes a purposeful God. God has a purpose for His creation, specifically for the pinnacle of His creation, people. And in our organizational context, He has purpose for business and work. The following verses from the Bible, although not exhaustive, attempt to be true to and accurately illustrate the storyline (or metanarrative) of the Bible to derive overall principles and values on this topic of Charter and purpose.

> The LORD has made everything for its purpose… (Proverbs 16:4a)

> And God blessed them. And God said to them, "Be fruitful and multiply and fill the earth and subdue it, and have dominion over the fish of the sea and over the birds of the heavens and over every living thing that moves on the earth." (Genesis 1:28)

> For his invisible attributes, namely, his eternal power and divine nature, have been clearly perceived, ever since the creation of the world, in the things that have been made. So they are without excuse. (Romans 1:20)

> For from him and through him and to him are all things. To him be glory forever. Amen. (Romans 11:36)

> And we know that for those who love God all things work together for good, for those who are called according to his purpose. (Romans 8:28)

> For we are his workmanship, created in Christ Jesus for good works, which God prepared beforehand, that we should walk in them. (Ephesians 2:10)

> I know that you can do all things, and that no purpose of yours can be thwarted. (Job 42:2)

> Do not be conformed to this world, but be transformed by the renewal of your mind, that by testing you may discern what is the will of God, what is good and acceptable and perfect. (Romans 12:2)

> He has told you, O man, what is good; and what does the LORD require of you but to do justice, and to love kindness, and to walk humbly with your God? (Micah 6:8)

For everything there is a season, and a time for every matter under heaven. (Ecclesiastes 3:1)

Everyone who is called by my name, whom I created for my glory, whom I formed and made. (Isaiah 43:7)

The Lord will fulfill his purpose for me; your steadfast love, O Lord, endures forever. Do not forsake the work of your hands. (Psalm 138:8)

So, whether you eat or drink, or whatever you do, do all to the glory of God. (1 Corinthians 10:31)

Then God said, "Let us make man in our image, after our likeness. And let them have dominion over the fish of the sea and over the birds of the heavens and over the livestock and over all the earth and over every creeping thing that creeps on the earth." (Genesis 1:26)

Many are the plans in the mind of a man, but it is the purpose of the Lord that will stand. (Proverbs 19:21)

But for this purpose I have raised you up, to show you my power, so that my name may be proclaimed in all the earth. (Exodus 9:16)

For I know the plans I have for you, declares the Lord, plans for welfare and not for evil, to give you a future and a hope. (Jeremiah 29:11)

The end of the matter; all has been heard. Fear God and keep his commandments, for this is the whole duty of man. For God will bring every deed into judgment, with every secret thing, whether good or evil. (Ecclesiastes 12:13–14)

Whatever you do, work heartily, as for the Lord and not for men, knowing that from the Lord you will receive the inheritance as your reward. You are serving the Lord Christ. (Colossians 3:23–24)

Let all that you do be done in love. (1 Corinthians 16:14)

Complete my joy by being of the same mind, having the same love, being in full accord and of one mind. Do nothing from selfish ambition or conceit, but in humility count others more significant than yourselves. Let each of you look not only to his own interests, but also to the interests of others. (Philippians 2:2–4)

Finally, all of you, have unity of mind, sympathy, brotherly love, a tender heart, and a humble mind. (1 Peter 3:8)

Whether these verses apply to creation in general, to all people for all time, or to a specific people for a specific time, we can see that God is purposeful and has purpose for His creation and for the people placed in creation to live and work. The Westminster Shorter Catechism summarizes the whole of the Bible regarding the purpose of people in the following question and answer:

Q: What is the chief end of man?

A: The chief end of man is to glorify God and to enjoy Him forever. [27]

Another way to state the purpose of life is to seek and allow God's continuing creation (grace) in ourselves and through our lives in the world. God created us for this and doing so glorifies Him.

---

27   Westminster Assembly, D. F. Kelly, P. B. Rollinson, and F. T. Marsh, *The Westminster Shorter Catechism in Modern English* (Phillipsburg, N.J: Presbyterian and Reformed Publishing, 1986).

Area 2: Leadership

Biblical Foundation

Throughout the Bible, we witness many leaders demonstrating Biblical leadership character and traits. The first and foremast character in the Bible to whom we should look first for leadership traits is Jesus. We can then look at others, including Paul, who clearly stated that we should follow him as he followed Jesus (1 Corinthians 11:1). We can also look at many others like Peter, John, Moses, Esther, Nehemiah, Ruth, Solomon, and others to compile a fairly comprehensive list of Biblical leadership characteristics we can use to lead Good Place organizations.

In Jesus's most famous speech, He clearly lays out character traits He values, and we should espouse them in our lives and, therefore, in our leadership. The speech has been called the Sermon on the Mount and is found in Matthew 5 through 7. In addition to the Sermon on the Mount, the following verses from the Bible, although not exhaustive, attempt to be true to and accurately illustrate the storyline (or metanarrative) of the Bible to derive overall principles and values on this topic of Leadership and the character of a leader.

> When he had washed their feet and put on his outer garments and resumed his place, he said to them, "Do you understand what I have done to you? You call me Teacher and Lord, and you are right, for so I am. If I then, your Lord and Teacher, have washed your feet, you also ought to wash one another's feet. For I have given you an example, that you also should do just as I have done to you." (John 13:12–15)

> Let no one despise you for your youth, but set the believers an example in speech, in conduct, in love, in faith, in purity. (1 Timothy 4:12)

> Do nothing from selfish ambition or conceit, but in humility count others more significant than yourselves. Let each of you look not only to his own interests, but also to the interests of others. (Philippians 2:3–4)

> Now the man Moses was very meek, more than all people who were on the face of the earth. (Numbers 12:3)

> I therefore, a prisoner for the Lord, urge you to walk in a manner worthy of the calling to which you have been called, with all humility and gentleness, with patience, bearing with one another in love. (Ephesians 4:1–2)

> For who sees anything different in you? What do you have that you did not receive? If then you received it, why do you boast as if you did not receive it? (1Corinthians 4:7)

> But he gives more grace. Therefore it says, "God opposes the proud but gives grace to the humble." (James 4:6)

Even as the Son of Man came not to be served but to serve, and to give his life as a ransom for many. (Matthew 20:28)

And Jesus called them to him and said to them, "You know that those who are considered rulers of the Gentiles lord it over them, and their great ones exercise authority over them. But it shall not be so among you. But whoever would be great among you must be your servant." (Mark 10:42–43)

And the Lord said, "Who then is the faithful and wise manager, whom his master will set over his household, to give them their portion of food at the proper time? Blessed is that servant whom his master will find so doing when he comes. Truly, I say to you, he will set him over all his possessions." (Luke 12:42–44)

Let love be genuine. Abhor what is evil; hold fast to what is good. Love one another with brotherly affection. Outdo one another in showing honor. (Romans 12:9–10)

And let us not grow weary of doing good, for in due season we will reap, if we do not give up. (Galatians 6:9)

Where there is no guidance, a people falls, but in an abundance of counselors there is safety. (Proverbs 11:14)

Not domineering over those in your charge, but being examples to the flock. (1 Peter 5:3)

With upright heart he shepherded them and guided them with his skillful hand. (Psalm 78:72)

Moreover, it is required of stewards that they be found faithful. (1 Corinthians 4:2)

That the man of God may be competent, equipped for every good work. (2 Timothy 3:17)

But the wisdom from above is first pure, then peaceable, gentle, open to reason, full of mercy and good fruits, impartial and sincere. (James 3:17)

How much better to get wisdom than gold! To get understanding is to be chosen rather than silver. (Proverbs 16:16)

The fear of the Lord is the beginning of wisdom, and the knowledge of the Holy One is insight. (Proverbs 9:10)

Knowing their thoughts, he said to them, "Every kingdom divided against itself is laid waste, and no city or house divided against itself will stand." (Matthew 12:25)

Let no corrupting talk come out of your mouths, but only such as is good for building up, as fits the occasion, that it may give grace to those who hear. (Ephesians 4:29)

But he knew their thoughts, and he said to the man with the withered hand, "Come and stand here." And he rose and stood there. (Luke 6:8)

But I discipline my body and keep it under control, lest after preaching to others I myself should be disqualified. (1 Corinthians 9:27)

Then the king said to me, "What are you requesting?" So I prayed to the God of heaven. And I said to the king, "If it pleases the king, and if your servant has found favor in your sight, that you send me to Judah, to the city of my fathers' graves, that I may rebuild it." (Nehemiah 2:4–5; and the story of Nehemiah)

Have I not commanded you? Be strong and courageous. Do not be frightened, and do not be dismayed, for the Lord your God is with you wherever you go." (Joshua 1:9)

But he would withdraw to desolate places and pray. (Luke 5:16)

But the fruit of the Spirit is love, joy, peace, patience, kindness, goodness, faithfulness, gentleness, self-control; against such things there is no law. (Galatians 5:22–23)

And we know that for those who love God all things work together for good, for those who are called according to his purpose. (Romans 8:28)

These verses demonstrate common themes of leadership characteristics from which we derive Good Place principles and values for leaders in the organization.

Area 3: Managing Systems

Biblical Foundation

We see in God's Word—both in the storyline of the Bible and in God's creation—systemic design, the idea that many individual and integrated parts are organized in a way that they become one and work together to accomplish a larger, common purpose. The Bible also illustrates this concept when describing the Church as many parts yet one body. The following verses from the Bible, although not exhaustive, attempt to be true to and accurately illustrate the storyline (or metanarrative) of the Bible to derive overall principles and values on this topic of Managing Systems.

> For just as the body is one and has many members, and all the members of the body, though many, are one body, so it is with Christ. (1 Corinthians 12:12)

> For the body does not consist of one member but of many. If the foot should say, "Because I am not a hand, I do not belong to the body," that would not make it any less a part of the body. And if the ear should say, "Because I am not an eye, I do not belong to the body," that would not make it any less a part of the body. If the whole body were an eye, where would be the sense of hearing? If the whole body were an ear, where would be the sense of smell? But as it is, God arranged the members in the body, each one of them, as he chose. If all were a single member, where would the body be? As it is, there are many parts, yet one body. The eye cannot say to the hand, "I have no need of you," nor again the head to the feet, "I have no need of you." On the contrary, the parts of the body that seem to be weaker are indispensable, and on those parts of the body that we think less honorable we bestow the greater honor, and our unpresentable parts are treated with greater modesty, which our more presentable parts do not require. But God has so composed the body, giving greater honor to the part that lacked it, that there may be no division in the body, but that the members may have the same care for one another. If one member suffers, all suffer together; if one member is honored, all rejoice together. (1 Corinthians 12:14–26)

> He is the image of the invisible God, the firstborn of all creation. For by him all things were created, in heaven and on earth, visible and invisible, whether thrones or dominions or rulers or authorities—all things were created through him and for him. And he is before all things, and in him all things hold together. And he is the head of the body, the church. He is the beginning, the firstborn from the dead, that in everything he might be preeminent. For in him all the fullness of God was pleased to dwell, and through him to reconcile to himself all things, whether on earth or in heaven, making peace by the blood of his cross. (Colossians 1:15–20)

I am the true vine, and my Father is the vinedresser. Every branch in me that does not bear fruit he takes away, and every branch that does bear fruit he prunes, that it may bear more fruit. Already you are clean because of the word that I have spoken to you. Abide in me, and I in you. As the branch cannot bear fruit by itself, unless it abides in the vine, neither can you, unless you abide in me. I am the vine; you are the branches. Whoever abides in me and I in him, he it is that bears much fruit, for apart from me you can do nothing. If anyone does not abide in me he is thrown away like a branch and withers; and the branches are gathered, thrown into the fire, and burned. If you abide in me, and my words abide in you, ask whatever you wish, and it will be done for you. By this my Father is glorified, that you bear much fruit and so prove to be my disciples. (John 15:1–8)

And I said to the king, "If it pleases the king, and if your servant has found favor in your sight, that you send me to Judah, to the city of my fathers' graves, that I may rebuild it." And the king said to me (the queen sitting beside him), "How long will you be gone, and when will you return?" So it pleased the king to send me when I had given him a time. And I said to the king, "If it pleases the king, let letters be given me to the governors of the province Beyond the River, that they may let me pass through until I come to Judah, and a letter to Asaph, the keeper of the king's forest, that he may give me timber to make beams for the gates of the fortress of the temple, and for the wall of the city, and for the house that I shall occupy." And the king granted me what I asked, for the good hand of my God was upon me. (Nehemiah 2:5–8, also see Nehemiah 2:1–4:23)

Now when the queen of Sheba heard of the fame of Solomon concerning the name of the Lord, she came to test him with hard questions. She came to Jerusalem with a very great retinue, with camels bearing spices and very much gold and precious stones. And when she came to Solomon, she told him all that was on her mind. And Solomon answered all her questions; there was nothing hidden from the king that he could not explain to her. And when the queen of Sheba had seen all the wisdom of Solomon, the house that he had built, the food of his table, the seating of his officials, and the attendance of his servants, their clothing, his cupbearers, and his burnt offerings that he offered at the house of the Lord, there was no more breath in her. And she said to the king, "The report was true that I heard in my own land of your words and of your wisdom, but I did not believe the reports until I came and my own eyes had seen it. And behold, the half was not told me. Your wisdom and prosperity surpass the report that I heard. Happy are your men! Happy are your servants, who continually stand before you and hear your wisdom! Blessed be the Lord your God, who has delighted in you and set you on the throne of Israel! Because the Lord loved Israel forever, he has made you king, that you may execute justice and righteousness." (1 Kings 10:1–9)

So God created man in his own image, in the image of God he created him; male and female he created them. And God blessed them. And God said to them, "Be fruitful and multiply and fill the earth and subdue it and have dominion over the fish of the sea and over the birds of the heavens and over every living thing that moves on the earth." And God said, "Behold, I have given you every plant yielding seed that is on the face of all the earth, and every tree with seed in its fruit. You shall have them for food. And to every beast of the earth and to every bird of the heavens and to everything that creeps on the earth, everything that has the breath of life, I have given every green plant for food." And it was so. (Genesis 1:27–30)

The earth is the Lord's and the fullness thereof, the world and those who dwell therein. (Psalm 24:1; see also Psalm 24:2–10)

As each has received a gift, use it to serve one another, as good stewards of God's varied grace. (1 Peter 4:10)

Whatever you do, work heartily, as for the Lord and not for men. (Colossians 3:23)

For it will be like a man going on a journey, who called his servants and entrusted to them his property. To one he gave five talents, to another two, to another one, to each according to his ability. Then he went away. He who had received the five talents went at once and traded with them, and he made five talents more. So also he who had the two talents made two talents more. But he who had received the one talent went and dug in the ground and hid his master's money. Now after a long time the master of those servants came and settled accounts with them. And he who had received the five talents came forward, bringing five talents more, saying, "Master, you delivered to me five talents; here, I have made five talents more." His master said to him, "Well done, good and faithful servant. You have been faithful over a little; I will set you over much. Enter into the joy of your master." And he also who had the two talents came forward, saying, "Master, you delivered to me two talents; here, I have made two talents more." His master said to him, "Well done, good and faithful servant. You have been faithful over a little; I will set you over much. Enter into the joy of your master." He also who had received the one talent came forward, saying, "Master, I knew you to be a hard man, reaping where you did not sow, and gathering where you scattered no seed, so I was afraid, and I went and hid your talent in the ground. Here, you have what is yours." But his master answered him, "You wicked and slothful servant! You knew that I reap where I have not sown and gather where I scattered no seed? Then you ought to have invested my money with the bankers, and at my coming I should have received what was my own with interest. So take the talent from him and give it to him who has the ten talents. For to everyone who has will more be given, and he will have an abundance. But from the one who has not, even what he has will be taken away." (Matthew 25:14–29)

So then each of us will give an account of himself to God. (Romans 14:12)

Having gifts that differ according to the grace given to us, let us use them . . . (Romans 12:6a)

We see in these verses that, first and foremost, God is Creator and Owner of all things. We, as human beings made in His image, are responsible and accountable to God to steward well that which He created and has given and entrusted to us to manage, tend, oversee, etc. We see that we are designed to work with and for a purpose and within a systematic context where we have a job yet do not just work for ourselves but work in connection with others for the betterment of each other and the world as co-creators and co-laborers with God. We were designed to work with excellence to grow and develop ourselves and others and bring glory to the Creator.

Area 4: Training, Education, and Development

Biblical Foundation

As we read throughout the Bible, the apex of God's creation is people. People are the only creation mentioned that are made in God's image. People are called to image God. People are also called to work (and do good works). Work is a means of grace through which we have the opportunity to image God and do what we are designed to do and fulfill our purpose, to glorify God, be fruitful, grow, and develop ourself and others into the people God designed us to become, to build society and culture, and to steward that which God has entrusted to the people He created. The following verses from the Bible, although not exhaustive, attempt to be true to and accurately illustrate the storyline (or metanarrative) of the Bible to derive overall principles and values on this topic of Training, Education, and Development.

> All Scripture is breathed out by God and profitable for teaching, for reproof, for correction, and for training in righteousness, that the man of God may be competent, equipped for every good work. (2 Timothy 3:16–17)

> Then God said, "Let us make man in our image, after our likeness. And let them have dominion over the fish of the sea and over the birds of the heavens and over the livestock and over all the earth and over every creeping thing that creeps on the earth." So God created man in his own image, in the image of God he created him; male and female he created them. (Genesis 1:26–27)

> Have nothing to do with irreverent, silly myths. Rather train yourself for godliness; for while bodily training is of some value, godliness is of value in every way, as it holds promise for the present life and also for the life to come. (1 Timothy 4:7–8)

> Do your best to present yourself to God as one approved, a worker who has no need to be ashamed, rightly handling the word of truth. (2 Timothy 2:15)

> For whatever was written in former days was written for our instruction, that through endurance and through the encouragement of the Scriptures we might have hope. (Romans 15:4)

> Do you not know that in a race all the runners run, but only one receives the prize? So run that you may obtain it. Every athlete exercises self-control in all things. They do it to receive a perishable wreath, but we an imperishable. So I do not run aimlessly; I do not box as one beating the air. But I discipline my body and keep it under control, lest after preaching to others I myself should be disqualified. (1 Corinthians 9:24–27)

> An athlete is not crowned unless he competes according to the rules. (2 Timothy 2:5)

A disciple is not above his teacher, but everyone when he is fully trained will be like his teacher. (Luke 6:40)

Or do you not know that your body is a temple of the Holy Spirit within you, whom you have from God? You are not your own, for you were bought with a price. So glorify God in your body. (1 Corinthians 6:19–20)

Do not be conformed to this world, but be transformed by the renewal of your mind, that by testing you may discern what is the will of God, what is good and acceptable and perfect. (Romans 12:2)

So, whether you eat or drink, or whatever you do, do all to the glory of God. (1 Corinthians 10:31)

For I know the plans I have for you, declares the Lord, plans for welfare and not for evil, to give you a future and a hope. (Jeremiah 29:11)

Whatever you do, work heartily, as for the Lord and not for men. (Colossians 3:23)

So as to walk in a manner worthy of the Lord, fully pleasing to him, bearing fruit in every good work and increasing in the knowledge of God. (Colossians 1:10)

And he answered, "You shall love the Lord your God with all your heart and with all your soul and with all your strength and with all your mind, and your neighbor as yourself." (Luke 10:27)

And let us not grow weary of doing good, for in due season we will reap, if we do not give up. (Galatians 6:9)

I appeal to you therefore, brothers, by the mercies of God, to present your bodies as a living sacrifice, holy and acceptable to God, which is your spiritual worship. Do not be conformed to this world, but be transformed by the renewal of your mind, that by testing you may discern what is the will of God, what is good and acceptable and perfect. (Romans 12:1–2)

Whatever your hand finds to do, do it with your might… (Ecclesiastes 9:10a)

An intelligent heart acquires knowledge, and the ear of the wise seeks knowledge. (Proverbs 18:15)

How much better to get wisdom than gold! To get understanding is to be chosen rather than silver. (Proverbs 16:16)

See to it that no one takes you captive by philosophy and empty deceit, according to human tradition, according to the elemental spirits of the world, and not according to Christ. (Colossians 2:8)

> Therefore, my beloved brothers, be steadfast, immovable, always abounding in the work of the Lord, knowing that in the Lord your labor is not in vain. (1 Corinthians 15:58)

> But grow in the grace and knowledge of our Lord and Savior Jesus Christ. To him be the glory both now and to the day of eternity. Amen. (2 Peter 3:18)

We see in these verses that the Bible is useful for teaching and training to be the people we are designed and intended to be, and to operate in a certain way that glorifies God and brings shalom to ourselves and those around us. In that, we are designed for work, for good works, and we have the opportunity to image God in all that we do and in and through the work that we do. We have the opportunity for work, which is a means of grace, to make us something better than we could on our own, making us into the people we can become in our work and in our lives, building up hearts of love and lives of shalom.

Area 5: Stewardship Planning

Biblical Foundation

The Bible has much to say about planning: why we plan, how we plan, what to expect when we plan, and some general guidelines around planning. There is a concept throughout the Bible that illustrates God's providence and our responsibility. He is sovereign and we are responsible. God created and owns all things. This plays a significant role in our responsibility to plan and our acknowledgment that God is totally sovereign in causing or allowing all things to come about, including the outcomes of those plans. In addition to what the Bible says about work, the following verses from the Bible, although not exhaustive, attempt to be true to and accurately illustrate the storyline (or metanarrative) of the Bible to derive overall principles and values on this topic of Stewardship Planning.

> And God blessed them. And God said to them, "Be fruitful and multiply and fill the earth and subdue it, and have dominion over the fish of the sea and over the birds of the heavens and over every living thing that moves on the earth." (Genesis 1:28)

> For it will be like a man going on a journey, who called his servants and entrusted to them his property. To one he gave five talents, to another two, to another one, to each according to his ability. Then he went away. He who had received the five talents went at once and traded with them, and he made five talents more. So also he who had the two talents made two talents more. But he who had received the one talent went and dug in the ground and hid his master's money. Now after a long time the master of those servants came and settled accounts with them. And he who had received the five talents came forward, bringing five talents more, saying, "Master, you delivered to me five talents; here, I have made five talents more." His master said to him, "Well done, good and faithful servant. You have been faithful over a little; I will set you over much. Enter into the joy of your master." And he also who had the two talents came forward, saying, "Master, you delivered to me two talents; here, I have made two talents more." His master said to him, "Well done, good and faithful servant. You have been faithful over a little; I will set you over much. Enter into the joy of your master." He also who had received the one talent came forward, saying, "'Master, I knew you to be a hard man, reaping where you did not sow, and gathering where you scattered no seed, so I was afraid, and I went and hid your talent in the ground. Here, you have what is yours." But his master answered him, "You wicked and slothful servant! You knew that I reap where I have not sown and gather where I scattered no seed? Then you ought to have invested my money with the bankers, and at my coming I should have received what was my own with interest. So take the talent from him and give it to him who has the ten talents. For to everyone who has will more be given, and he will have an abundance. But from the one who has not, even what he has will be taken away." (Matthew 25:14–29)

For by him all things were created, in heaven and on earth, visible and invisible, whether thrones or dominions or rulers or authorities—all things were created through him and for him. (Colossians 1:16)

But seek first the kingdom of God and his righteousness, and all these things will be added to you. (Matthew 6:33)

Commit your work to the Lord, and your plans will be established. (Proverbs 16:3)

For my thoughts are not your thoughts, neither are your ways my ways, declares the Lord. For as the heavens are higher than the earth, so are my ways higher than your ways and my thoughts than your thoughts. (Isaiah 55:8–9)

The heart of man plans his way, but the Lord establishes his steps. (Proverbs 16:9)

Desire without knowledge is not good, and whoever makes haste with his feet misses his way. (Proverbs 19:2)

Do not be anxious about anything, but in everything by prayer and supplication with thanksgiving let your requests be made known to God. (Philippians 4:6)

Many are the plans in the mind of a man, but it is the purpose of the Lord that will stand. (Proverbs 19:21)

The plans of the diligent lead surely to abundance, but everyone who is hasty comes only to poverty. (Proverbs 21:5)

By wisdom a house is built, and by understanding it is established; by knowledge the rooms are filled with all precious and pleasant riches. (Proverbs 24:3–4)

Wealth gained hastily will dwindle, but whoever gathers little by little will increase it. (Proverbs 13:11)

For which of you, desiring to build a tower, does not first sit down and count the cost, whether he has enough to complete it? Otherwise, when he has laid a foundation and is not able to finish, all who see it begin to mock him, saying, "This man began to build and was not able to finish." (Luke 14:28–30)

One who is faithful in a very little is also faithful in much, and one who is dishonest in a very little is also dishonest in much. (Luke 16:10)

Come now, you who say, "Today or tomorrow we will go into such and such a town and spend a year there and trade and make a profit"—yet you do not know what tomorrow will bring. What is your life? For you are a mist that appears for a little time and then vanishes. Instead, you ought to say, "If the Lord wills, we will live and do this or that." (James 4:13–15)

Where there is no guidance, a people falls, but in an abundance of counselors there is safety. (Proverbs 11:14)

No one can serve two masters, for either he will hate the one and love the other, or he will be devoted to the one and despise the other. You cannot serve God and money. (Matthew 6:24)

And he told them a parable, saying, "The land of a rich man produced plentifully, and he thought to himself, 'What shall I do, for I have nowhere to store my crops?' And he said, 'I will do this: I will tear down my barns and build larger ones, and there I will store all my grain and my goods. And I will say to my soul, "Soul, you have ample goods laid up for many years; relax, eat, drink, be merry."' But God said to him, 'Fool! This night your soul is required of you, and the things you have prepared, whose will they be?' So is the one who lays up treasure for himself and is not rich toward God." (Luke 12:16–21)

But he who is noble plans noble things, and on noble things he stands. (Isaiah 32:8)

Trust in the Lord with all your heart, and do not lean on your own understanding. In all your ways acknowledge him, and he will make straight your paths. (Proverbs 3:5–6)

The point is this: whoever sows sparingly will also reap sparingly, and whoever sows bountifully will also reap bountifully. Each one must give as he has decided in his heart, not reluctantly or under compulsion, for God loves a cheerful giver. (2 Corinthians 9:6–7)

As each has received a gift, use it to serve one another, as good stewards of God's varied grace. (1 Peter 4:10)

Whatever you do, work heartily, as for the Lord and not for men, knowing that from the Lord you will receive the inheritance as your reward. You are serving the Lord Christ. (Colossians 3:23–24)

And we know that for those who love God all things work together for good, for those who are called according to his purpose. (Romans 8:28)

In these verses we see that we have a responsibility to plan. We are to seek God's Kingdom and His purposes in those plans. We are to trust, acknowledge, and commit our plans to the Lord. We are to be guided by Biblical wisdom and discernment. We are to use good information and knowledge. We are to be unselfish, generous, and diligent; not greedy, prideful, or anxious. Lastly, we are to be good stewards of the gifts and resources we have been given to bring about a good return based on Biblical success criteria.

Area 6: Financial Management

Biblical Foundation

Money is one of the most significant topics mentioned in the Bible. Some have calculated it is the second most referred to topic in the Bible with over 2,000 related verses throughout Scripture. The following verses are but a small sample and, although not exhaustive by any means, attempt to be true to and accurately illustrate the storyline (or metanarrative) of the Bible to derive overall principles and values on this topic of Financial Management:

> No one can serve two masters, for either he will hate the one and love the other, or he will be devoted to the one and despise the other. You cannot serve God and money. (Matthew 6:24)

> For the love of money is a root of all kinds of evils . . . (1 Timothy 6:10a)

> Keep your life free from love of money, and be content with what you have, for he has said, "I will never leave you nor forsake you." (Hebrews 13:5)

> Wealth gained hastily will dwindle, but whoever gathers little by little will increase it. (Proverbs 13:11)

> Behold, the wages of the laborers who mowed your fields, which you kept back by fraud, are crying out against you, and the cries of the harvesters have reached the ears of the Lord of hosts. (James 5:4)

> For the Scripture says, "You shall not muzzle an ox when it treads out the grain," and, "The laborer deserves his wages." (1 Timothy 5:18)

> Whoever oppresses the poor to increase his own wealth, or gives to the rich, will only come to poverty. (Proverbs 22:16)

> Whatever you do, work heartily, as for the Lord and not for men. (Colossians 3:23)

> And my God will supply every need of yours according to his riches in glory in Christ Jesus. (Philippians 4:19)

> He who loves money will not be satisfied with money, nor he who loves wealth with his income; this also is vanity. (Ecclesiastes 5:10)

And he said to them, "Take care, and be on your guard against all covetousness, for one's life does not consist in the abundance of his possessions." (Luke 12:15)

Honor the Lord with your wealth and with the first fruits of all your produce; then your barns will be filled with plenty, and your vats will be bursting with wine. (Proverbs 3:9–10)

Do not lay up for yourselves treasures on earth, where moth and rust destroy and where thieves break in and steal, but lay up for yourselves treasures in heaven, where neither moth nor rust destroys and where thieves do not break in and steal. For where your treasure is, there your heart will be also. (Matthew 6:19–21)

For which of you, desiring to build a tower, does not first sit down and count the cost, whether he has enough to complete it? Otherwise, when he has laid a foundation and is not able to finish, all who see it begin to mock him, saying, "This man began to build and was not able to finish." (Luke 14:28–30)

As each has received a gift, use it to serve one another, as good stewards of God's varied grace. (1 Peter 4:10)

The point is this: whoever sows sparingly will also reap sparingly, and whoever sows bountifully will also reap bountifully. Each one must give as he has decided in his heart, not reluctantly or under compulsion, for God loves a cheerful giver. (2 Corinthians 9:6–7)

But if anyone does not provide for his relatives, and especially for members of his household, he has denied the faith and is worse than an unbeliever. (1 Timothy 5:8)

In all things I have shown you that by working hard in this way we must help the weak and remember the words of the Lord Jesus, how he himself said, "It is more blessed to give than to receive." (Acts 20:35)

John answered, "A person cannot receive even one thing unless it is given him from heaven." (John 3:27)

I, wisdom, dwell with prudence, and I find knowledge and discretion. (Proverbs 8:12)

The prudent sees danger and hides himself, but the simple go on and suffer for it. (Proverbs 27:12)

The rich rules over the poor, and the borrower is the slave of the lender. (Proverbs 22:7)

For it will be like a man going on a journey, who called his servants and entrusted to them his property. To one he gave five talents, to another two, to another one, to each according to his ability. Then he went away. He who had received the five talents went at once and traded with them, and he made five talents more. So also he who had the two talents made two talents more. But he who had received the one talent went and dug in the ground and hid his master's money. Now after a long time the master of those servants came and settled accounts with them. And he who had received the five talents came forward, bringing five talents more, saying, "Master, you delivered to me five talents; here, I have made five talents more." His master said to him, "Well done, good and faithful servant. You have been faithful over a little; I will set you over much. Enter into the joy of your master." And he also who had the two talents came forward, saying, "Master, you delivered to me two talents; here, I have made two talents more." His master said to him, "Well done, good and faithful servant. You have been faithful over a little; I will set you over much. Enter into the joy of your master." He also who had received the one talent came forward, saying, "Master, I knew you to be a hard man, reaping where you did not sow, and gathering where you scattered no seed, so I was afraid, and I went and hid your talent in the ground. Here, you have what is yours." But his master answered him, "You wicked and slothful servant! You knew that I reap where I have not sown and gather where I scattered no seed? Then you ought to have invested my money with the bankers, and at my coming I should have received what was my own with interest. So take the talent from him and give it to him who has the ten talents. For to everyone who has will more be given, and he will have an abundance. But from the one who has not, even what he has will be taken away." (Matthew 25:14–29)

Then he said to them, "Therefore render to Caesar the things that are Caesar's, and to God the things that are God's." (Matthew 22:21b)

The earth is the Lord's and the fullness thereof, the world and those who dwell therein. (Psalm 24:1)

In these verses, we see emerging themes about money and finances. As with all created things, God is the ultimate Owner, Provider, and Giver of good gifts. We are called to steward that which He provides in a way that represents the Owner's purposes and desires for His creation. Money is no different, except money (specifically the motivation for money and for the benefits the world bestows on those who attain more of it) seems be one of those things, like power and sex, that have a tremendous pull on our hearts and seems to have a significant and unique allure for our attention and for the place of God in our lives. These verses address the place money should have in our lives, including the purpose it serves, the motivation for it, how we attain it, and the investment and good use of it.

Area 7: Managing Innovation

Biblical Foundation

The following verses from the Bible, although not exhaustive, attempt to be true to and accurately illustrate the storyline (or metanarrative) of the Bible to derive overall principles and values on this topic of Managing Innovation.

> In the beginning, God created the heavens and the earth. (Genesis 1:1; also see Genesis 1:1–31)

> Then God said, "Let us make man in our image, after our likeness. And let them have dominion over the fish of the sea and over the birds of the heavens and over the livestock and over all the earth and over every creeping thing that creeps on the earth." So God created man in his own image, in the image of God he created him; male and female he created them. (Genesis 1:26–27)

> Then the Lord God formed the man of dust from the ground and breathed into his nostrils the breath of life, and the man became a living creature. (Genesis 2:7)

> For by him all things were created, in heaven and on earth, visible and invisible, whether thrones or dominions or rulers or authorities—all things were created through him and for him. (Colossians 1:16)

> And God blessed them. And God said to them, "Be fruitful and multiply and fill the earth and subdue it, and have dominion over the fish of the sea and over the birds of the heavens and over every living thing that moves on the earth." (Genesis 1:28)

> Behold, the days are coming, declares the Lord, when I will make a new covenant with the house of Israel and the house of Judah, not like the covenant that I made with their fathers on the day when I took them by the hand to bring them out of the land of Egypt, my covenant that they broke, though I was their husband, declares the Lord. For this is the covenant that I will make with the house of Israel after those days, declares the Lord: I will put my law within them, and I will write it on their hearts. And I will be their God, and they shall be my people. (Jeremiah 31:31–33)

> Worthy are you, our Lord and God, to receive glory and honor and power, for you created all things, and by your will they existed and were created. (Revelation 4:11)

> From now on, therefore, we regard no one according to the flesh. Even though we once regarded Christ according to the flesh, we regard him thus no longer. Therefore, if anyone is in Christ, he is a new creation. The old has passed away; behold, the new has come. All this is from God, who through

Christ reconciled us to himself and gave us the ministry of reconciliation; that is, in Christ God was reconciling the world to himself, not counting their trespasses against them, and entrusting to us the message of reconciliation. (2 Corinthians 5:16–19)

To put off your old self, which belongs to your former manner of life and is corrupt through deceitful desires, and to be renewed in the spirit of your minds, and to put on the new self, created after the likeness of God in true righteousness and holiness. (Ephesians 4:22–24)

And he who was seated on the throne said, "Behold, I am making all things new." Also, he said, "Write this down, for these words are trustworthy and true." (Revelation 21:5)

Again, we see in these verses that God is the Creator of the world and everything in it. He is the original Creator and Innovator of new things. We see that we are made in His image and thus have been given the privilege and opportunity of co-creating and innovating as God's image bearers.

Area 8: Managing Internal and External Communication

Biblical Foundation

The following verses from the Bible, although not exhaustive, attempt to be true to and accurately illustrate the storyline (or metanarrative) of the Bible to derive overall principles and values on this topic of Communication.

> Let no corrupting talk come out of your mouths, but only such as is good for building up, as fits the occasion, that it may give grace to those who hear. (Ephesians 4:29)

> Know this, my beloved brothers: let every person be quick to hear, slow to speak, slow to anger. (James 1:19)

> Therefore encourage one another and build one another up, just as you are doing. (1 Thessalonians 5:11)

> When words are many, transgression is not lacking, but whoever restrains his lips is prudent. (Proverbs 10:19)

> There is one whose rash words are like sword thrusts, but the tongue of the wise brings healing. (Proverbs 12:18)

> A soft answer turns away wrath, but a harsh word stirs up anger. (Proverbs 15:1)

> If one gives an answer before he hears, it is his folly and shame. (Proverbs 18:13)

> Death and life are in the power of the tongue, and those who love it will eat its fruits. (Proverbs 18:21)

> Let the words of my mouth and the meditation of my heart be acceptable in your sight, O Lord, my rock and my redeemer. (Psalm 19:14)

> Rather, speaking the truth in love, we are to grow up in every way into him who is the head, into Christ. (Ephesians 4:15)

> Let your speech always be gracious, seasoned with salt, so that you may know how you ought to answer each person. (Colossians 4:6)

> All Scripture is breathed out by God and profitable for teaching, for reproof, for correction, and for training in righteousness. (2 Timothy 3:16)

> Set a guard, O Lord, over my mouth; keep watch over the door of my lips! (Psalm 141:3)

The tongue of the wise commends knowledge, but the mouths of fools pour out folly. (Proverbs 15:2)

Whoever keeps his mouth and his tongue keeps himself out of trouble. (Proverbs 21:23)

But avoid irreverent babble, for it will lead people into more and more ungodliness. (2 Timothy 2:16)

Therefore, having put away falsehood, let each one of you speak the truth with his neighbor, for we are members one of another. (Ephesians 4:25)

A word fitly spoken is like apples of gold in a setting of silver. (Proverbs 25:11)

In these verses, we see themes of communication such as being quick to hear and slow to speak including being thoughtful with our words and appropriate for the audience and the situation. We also see what type of communication we should be focusing on, that communication that is truthful, loving, wise, gracious, encouraging, not harsh or rash, intentional, building up, and unifying. We should be speaking words of life versus words of death.

Area 9: Managing the Business Formula

Biblical Foundation

The following verses from the Bible, although not exhaustive, attempt to be true to and accurately illustrate the storyline (or metanarrative) of the Bible to derive overall principles and values on this topic of Managing the Business Formula. You will notice that we have seen these verses in earlier sections of *The 10 Areas*. The reason why should become obvious in the Practical Application section.

> For by him all things were created, in heaven and on earth, visible and invisible, whether thrones or dominions or rulers or authorities—all things were created through him and for him. (Colossians 1:16)

> Then God said, "Let us make man in our image, after our likeness. And let them have dominion over the fish of the sea and over the birds of the heavens and over the livestock and over all the earth and over every creeping thing that creeps on the earth." So God created man in his own image, in the image of God he created him; male and female he created them. (Genesis 1:26–27)

> The Lord has made everything for its purpose… (Proverbs 16:4a)

> For his invisible attributes, namely, his eternal power and divine nature, have been clearly perceived, ever since the creation of the world, in the things that have been made. So they are without excuse. (Romans 1:20)

> For from him and through him and to him are all things. To him be glory forever. Amen. (Romans 11:36)

> The Lord will fulfill his purpose for me; your steadfast love, O Lord, endures forever. Do not forsake the work of your hands. (Psalm 138:8)

> For we are his workmanship, created in Christ Jesus for good works, which God prepared beforehand, that we should walk in them. (Ephesians 2:10)

> Do not be conformed to this world, but be transformed by the renewal of your mind, that by testing you may discern what is the will of God, what is good and acceptable and perfect. (Romans 12:2)

> The end of the matter; all has been heard. Fear God and keep his commandments, for this is the whole duty of man. For God will bring every deed into judgment, with every secret thing, whether good or evil. (Ecclesiastes 12:13–14)

> He has told you, O man, what is good; and what does the Lord require of you but to do justice, and to love kindness, and to walk humbly with your God? (Micah 6:8)

Let all that you do be done in love. (1 Corinthians 16:14)

Do nothing from selfish ambition or conceit, but in humility count others more significant than yourselves. Let each of you look not only to his own interests, but also to the interests of others. (Philippians 2:3–4)

But he gives more grace. Therefore it says, "God opposes the proud but gives grace to the humble." (James 4:6)

And the Lord said, "Who then is the faithful and wise manager, whom his master will set over his household, to give them their portion of food at the proper time? Blessed is that servant whom his master will find so doing when he comes. Truly, I say to you, he will set him over all his possessions. (Luke 12:42–44)

Let love be genuine. Abhor what is evil; hold fast to what is good. Love one another with brotherly affection. Outdo one another in showing honor. (Romans 12:9–10)

Where there is no guidance, a people falls, but in an abundance of counselors there is safety. (Proverbs 11:14)

How much better to get wisdom than gold! To get understanding is to be chosen rather than silver. (Proverbs 16:16)

But the fruit of the Spirit is love, joy, peace, patience, kindness, goodness, faithfulness, gentleness, self-control; against such things there is no law. (Galatians 5:22–23)

For just as the body is one and has many members, and all the members of the body, though many, are one body, so it is with Christ. (1 Corinthians 12:12; also see 1 Corinthians 12:12–26)

As it is, there are many parts, yet one body. (1 Corinthians 12:20)

And we know that for those who love God all things work together for good, for those who are called according to his purpose. (Romans 8:28)

As each has received a gift, use it to serve one another, as good stewards of God's varied grace. (1 Peter 4:10)

Having gifts that differ according to the grace given to us, let us use them … (Romans 12:6a)

In these verses, as we experienced in previous sections, we see that God is Creator and Owner of all things. He has created all things with purpose. We see He has created the natural world to work together to fulfill His purposes. We see that, as people created in God's image and through God's grace, we have been given different and unique gifts to be used for good works. We are to steward those different and unique gifts with wisdom, discernment, and according to God's ways and intentions for a life of love, peace, patience, kindness, goodness, faithfulness, gentleness, self-control, and shalom. We also see that God has established behavioral values for our good that should guide us in how live in this world, how we view ourselves, how we view and interact with one another, how we view and interact with the world around us, and how we perceive ourselves in all these interactions. All of these many parts are to work together in unity to serve God and one another, stewarding that which He has given us to fulfill His good purposes.

Area 10: Community Engagement

Biblical Foundation

The following verses from the Bible, although not exhaustive, attempt to be true to and accurately illustrate the storyline (or metanarrative) of the Bible to derive overall principles and values on this topic of Community Engagement.

> Pray then like this: "Our Father in heaven, hallowed be your name. Your kingdom come, your will be done, on earth as it is in heaven. (Matthew 6:9–10)

> And he said to him, "You shall love the Lord your God with all your heart and with all your soul and with all your mind. This is the great and first commandment. And a second is like it: You shall love your neighbor as yourself." (Matthew 22:37–39)

> As each has received a gift, use it to serve one another, as good stewards of God's varied grace. (1 Peter 4:10)

> And let us consider how to stir up one another to love and good works. (Hebrews 10:24)

> For we are his workmanship, created in Christ Jesus for good works, which God prepared beforehand, that we should walk in them. (Ephesians 2:10)

> But seek the welfare of the city where I have sent you into exile, and pray to the Lord on its behalf, for in its welfare you will find your welfare. (Jeremiah 29:7)

> "Which of these three, do you think, proved to be a neighbor to the man who fell among the robbers?" He said, "The one who showed him mercy." And Jesus said to him, "You go, and do likewise." (Luke 10:36–37)

> And God blessed them. And God said to them, "Be fruitful and multiply and fill the earth and subdue it, and have dominion over the fish of the sea and over the birds of the heavens and over every living thing that moves on the earth." (Genesis 1:28)

> And as he reclined at table in his house, many tax collectors and sinners were reclining with Jesus and his disciples, for there were many who followed him. And the scribes of the Pharisees, when they saw that he was eating with sinners and tax collectors, said to his disciples, "Why does he eat with tax collectors and sinners?" And when Jesus heard it, he said to them, "Those who are well have no need of a physician, but those who are sick. I came not to call the righteous, but sinners." (Mark 2:15–17)

And Jesus came and said to them, "All authority in heaven and on earth has been given to me. Go therefore and make disciples of all nations, baptizing them in the name of the Father and of the Son and of the Holy Spirit, teaching them to observe all that I have commanded you. And behold, I am with you always, to the end of the age." (Matthew 28:18–20)

Then Jesus said to him, "Put your sword back into its place. For all who take the sword will perish by the sword. Do you think that I cannot appeal to my Father, and he will at once send me more than twelve legions of angels? But how then should the Scriptures be fulfilled, that it must be so?" (Matthew 26:52–54)

Jesus answered, "My kingdom is not of this world. If my kingdom were of this world, my servants would have been fighting, that I might not be delivered over to the Jews. But my kingdom is not from the world." (John 18:36)

Therefore, we are ambassadors for Christ, God making his appeal through us. We implore you on behalf of Christ, be reconciled to God. (2 Corinthians 5:20)

In these verses and many more like them, we see that we are called to love God and love others, and to bring God's Kingdom and those Kingdom characteristics here on earth in every sphere of life. We are given gifts and called to serve one another and pray for people's welfare, stirring each other up to love and good works, providing for each other's needs. We are God's ambassadors, representatives to model and help bring about the kind of life and experiences He intends and we were designed for.

We also see how Jesus interacts with people in the community, where He meets people in their current and humble state, serves them, meets their deepest needs, and, in non-forcible manner, calls and provides a way for people to experience His heart of love and His shalom.

BIBLIOGRAPHY

Carver, John. *Boards that Make a Difference. 3rd ed.* Hoboken, NJ: Jossey-Bass, 2006.

Carver, John, and Miriam Carver. *Reinventing Your Board. Rev. ed.* Hoboken, NJ: Jossey-Bass, 2006.

Cooperrider, D. and D. Whitney. *Appreciative Inquiry: A Positive Revolution in Change.* Oakland, CA: Berrett-Koehler Publishers, 2005.

Deming, W. Edwards. *Out of the Crisis.* Cambridge, MA: MIT Press, 2018.

Deming, W. Edwards. *The New Economics for Industry, Government, Education. 2nd ed.* Cambridge, MA: MIT Press, 1994.

Doerr, J. Measure What Matters: *How Google, Bono, and the Gates Foundation Rock the World with OKR's.* New York: Portfolio/Penguin, 2018.

The Guinness Book of World Records. Stamford, CT: Guinness Media, 1997. Guinness Book of World Records.com. https://www.guinnessworldrecords.com/world-records/best-selling-book-of-non-fiction.

Kaplan R. and D. Norton. *The Balanced Scorecard: Translating Strategy into Action.* Brighton, MA: Harvard Business Review Press, 1996.

Lencioni, Patrick. *The Advantage: Why Organizational Health Trumps Everything Else in Business.* Hoboken, NJ: Jossey-Bass, 2012.

Mangalwadi, V. *The Book that Made Your World: How the Bible Created the Soul of Western Civilization.* Nashville: Thomas Nelson, 2011.

Miller, Calvin. *Into the Depths of God: Where Eyes See the Invisible, Ears Hear the Inaudible, and Minds Conceive the Inconceivable.* Bloomington, MN: Bethany House, 2000.

Myers, Scott. *The Eutopia Book: 0 Introduction.* Tallmadge, OH: Good Place Publishing, 2017.

Myers, Scott. *The Eutopia Book: 1 Communities.* Tallmadge, OH: Good Place Publishing, 2017.

Myers, Scott. *The Eutopia Book: 2 Individual.* Tallmadge, OH: Good Place Publishing, 2017.

Myers, Scott. *The Eutopia Book: 3 Organizations.* Tallmadge, OH: Good Place Publishing, 2017.

Myers, Scott. *Finding Value: The Art of Life in Organizations.* Akron, OH: Eutopia Report, Inc, 2005.

Sinek, Simon. *Start with Why: How Great Leaders Inspire Everyone to Take Action.* New York: Portfolio, 2009.

Welchel, Hugh. *"The Historical Influences of the Sacred-Secular Divide."* Institute for Faith, Work, & Economics. October 17, 2016. https://tifwe.org/historical-influences-of-the-sacred-secular-divide.

Welchel, Hugh. *How Then Should We Work.* McLean, VA: WestBow Press, 2012.

Westminster Assembly, D. F. Kelly, P. B. Rollinson, and F. T. Marsh. *The Westminster Shorter Catechism in Modern English.* Phillipsburg, NJ: Presbyterian and Reformed Publishing, 1986.

Wickman, G. Traction: *Get a Grip on Your Business.* Dallas: BenBella Books, 2012.